GREEK ART

Author: Elie Faure and Klaus H. Carl

Layout:
Baseline Co. Ltd,
232/17 Vo Thi Sau Street
4th Floor
District 3, Ho Chi Minh City
Vietnam

ISBN: 978-1-68325-924-4

Printed in

Elie Faure and Klaus H. Carl

GREEK ART

The Birthplace of Beauty and Classical Ideals

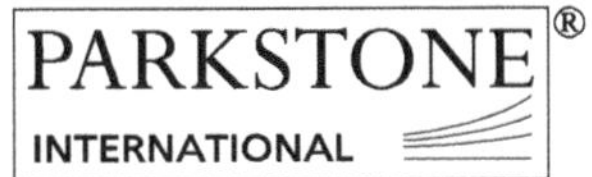

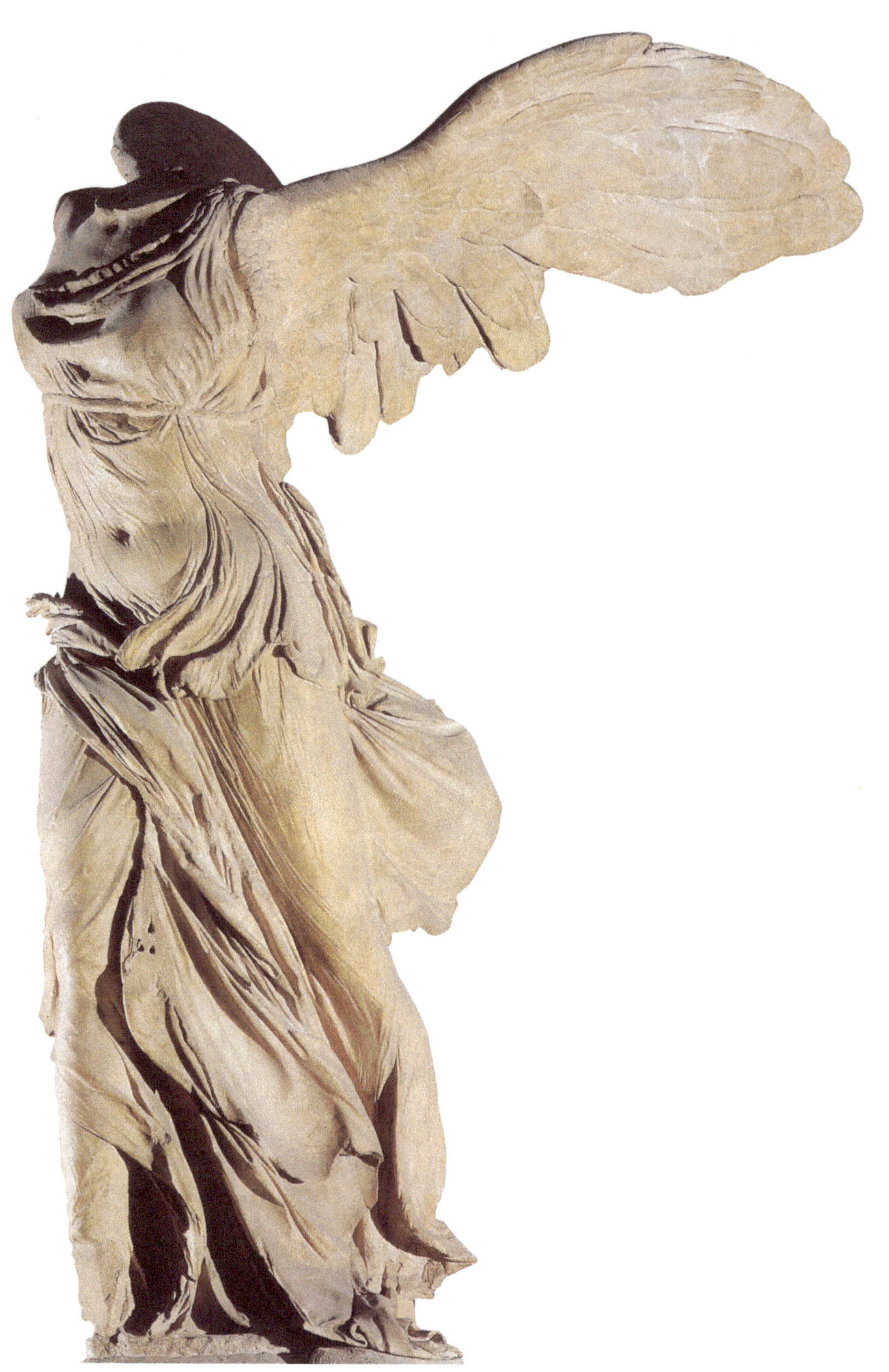

CONTENTS

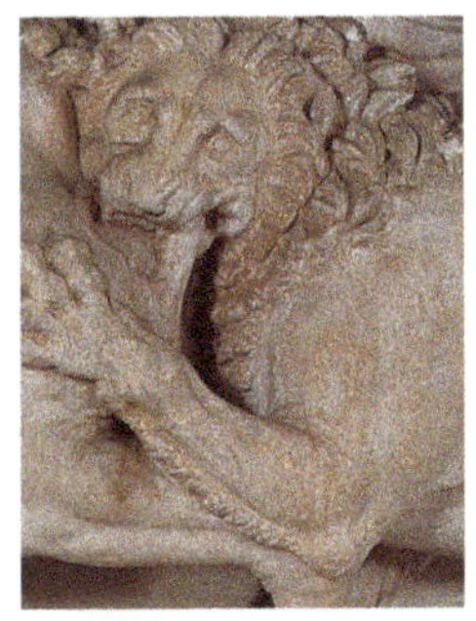
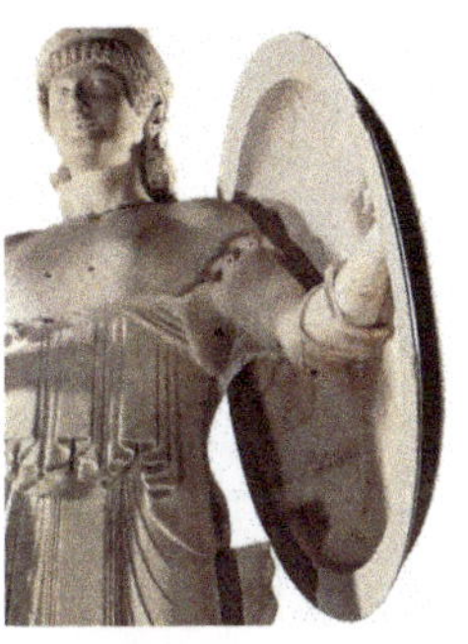
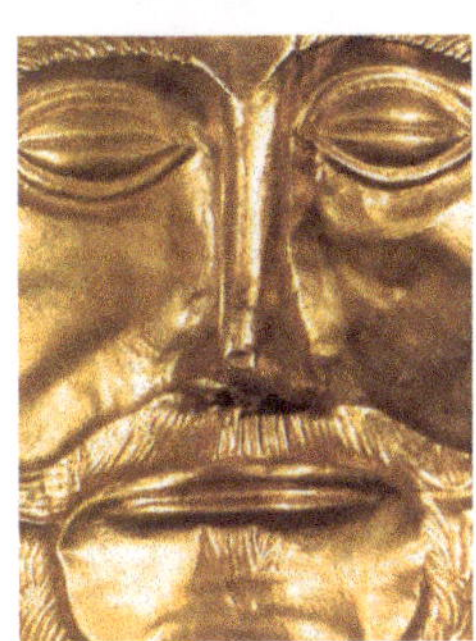
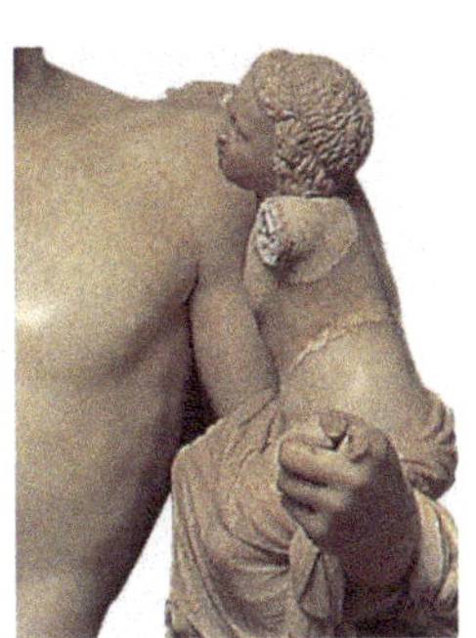
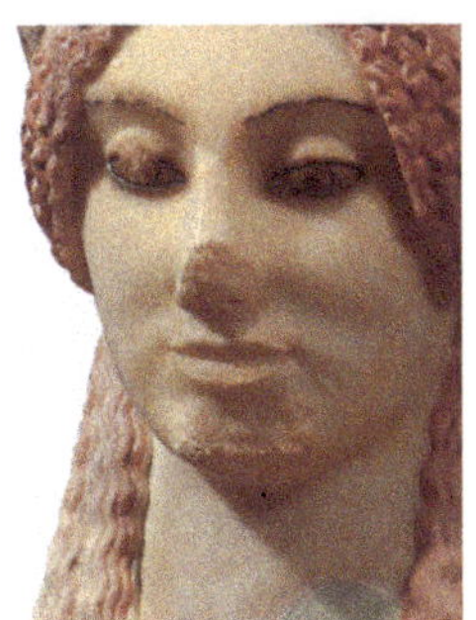

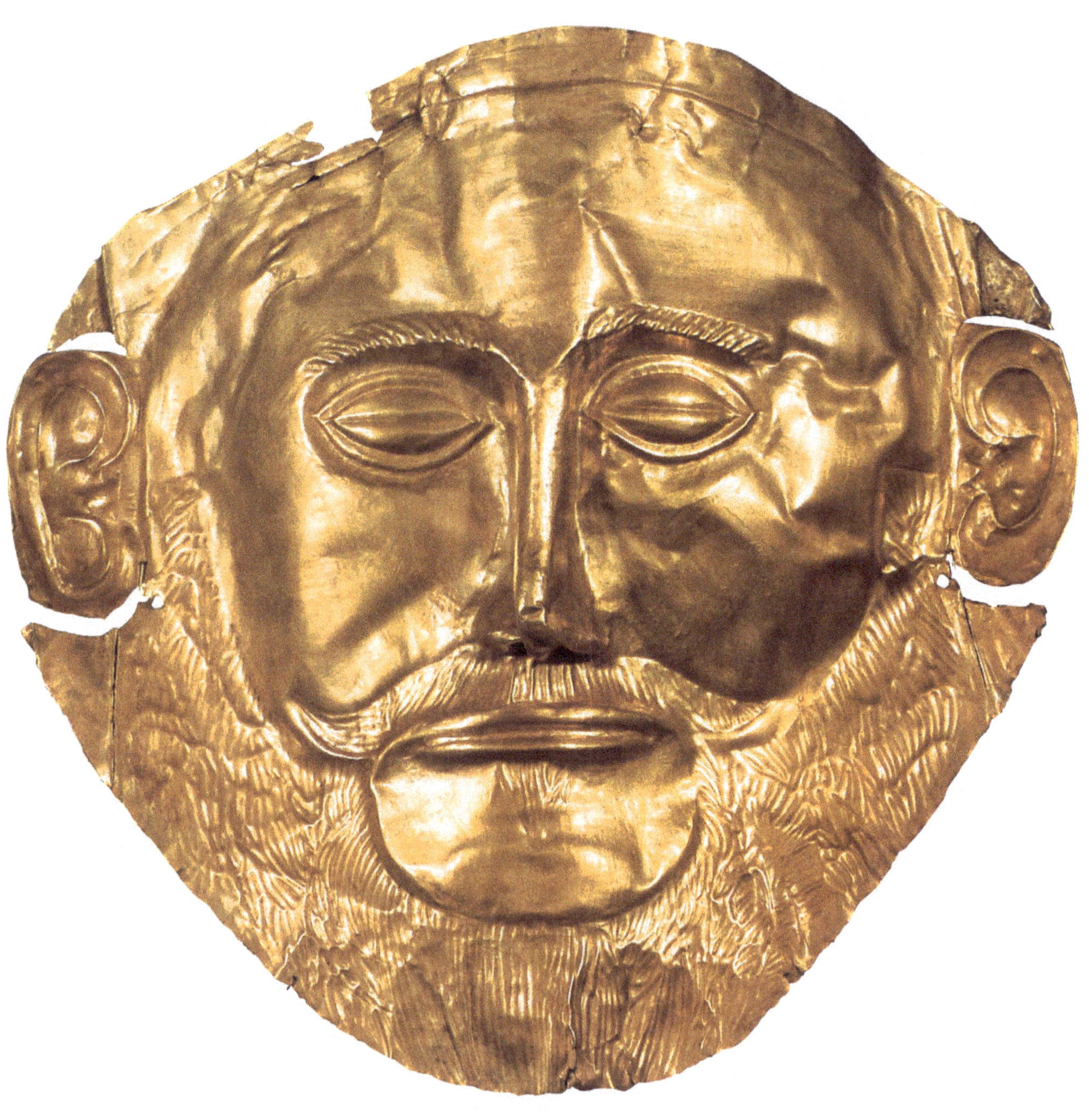

INTRODUCTION

From fishing, coast trade, the small business of one isle with another, from rapine and piracy, a whole little moving world of sailors, merchants, and corsairs lived their healthy life, neither a rich nor a poor one — a mean one — if we think of the vast commercial enterprises and the great explorations which the Phoenicians undertook. Their feet in the water and their faces to the wind, the men of the Aegean would carry to the traffickers from Tyre and Sidon who had just entered the port, under blue, green, and red sails, their fish and their olives in vases painted with marine plants, octopuses, seaweed, and other forms taken from the teeming, viscous life of the deep. It needed centuries, doubtless, for the tribes of a single island or a single coast to recognize a chief, to consent to follow him afar on cunning and bloody expeditions to the cities of the continent, whence they brought back jewels, golden vessels, rich stuffs, and women. And it was only then that the Achaeans and the Danai of the old poems heaped up those heavy stones on the fortified promontories, the Cyclopean walls, the Pelasgic walls under the shadow of which the Atreides, crowned with gold like the barbarian kings who sallied forth from the forests of the north two thousand years later, sat at table before the meats and wines, with their friends and their soldiers.

Such origins could only make them subtle and hard. Aeschylus (c. 525/524 – c. 456/455 BC) felt this when he came there, after eight centuries, to listen in the solitude to the echo of the death cries of the frightful family. These pirates selected sites for their lair near the sea — tragically consistent with their life of murder and the heavy orgies which followed upon their deeds of crime. A circle of hills — bare, devoured by fire and enlivened by no torrent, no tree, no bird cry. We find the life of these men depicted on the sides of the rudely chiseled vase of Vaphio (ancient site in Laconia, Greece), and on the strips of wall remaining beneath the ruins of Tirynth and of Knossos. There are bits of frescoes there as free as the flight of the sea birds; the art is of a terrible candor, but is already disintegrating. One sees women with bare breasts, rouge on their lips, black around the eyes, their flounced dresses betraying the bad taste of the barbarian; they are painted and sophisticated

▲ **The Winged Victory of Samothrace,**
also called the Nike of Samothrace, c. 200 – 190 B.C.
Parian marble Louvre, Paris.

◄ **The Mask of Agamemnon,**
funeral mask, c. 1550–1500 B.C., Gold
National Archaeological Museum, Athens.

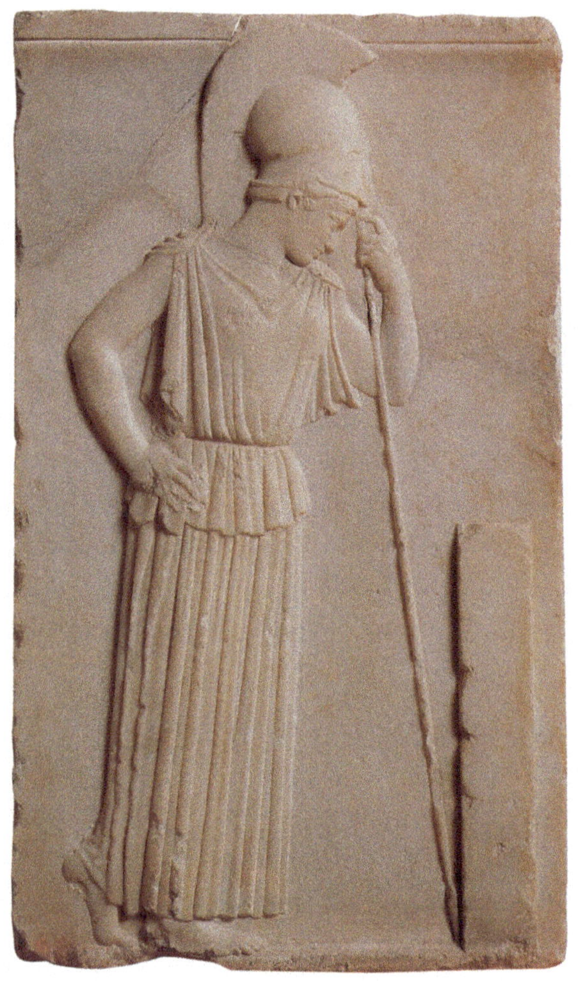

▲ **The Contemplative Athena Relief,** 460 B.C.
Marble, h: 54 cm
Acropolis Museum, Athens

dolls bought in the Orient or taken by force on the expeditions of violence.

Here are bulls pursued in the olive groves, bulls galloping, rearing, charging upon men or tangled in great nets. Sometimes there are reapers who laugh and sing with tremendous gaiety among the sheaves of wheat which they carry, but usually we find the questionable woman, the wild beast, and the marine monster; a voluptuous and brutal life like that of every primitive man rose to a post of command by force or by chance. As guardians of the gates of their acropolis they set up stone lionesses with bronze heads, heavily erect. When they died these men were laid away in a shroud of gold leaf.

It was a civilization already rotten, a Byzantium in miniature, where dramas of the bedroom determined revolutions and massacres. It ended like the others. The Dorian descends from the north like an avalanche, rolls over Argolis and even to Crete, devastating the cities and razing the acropolises. Legendary Greece enters a thick darkness from which she would not have reappeared if the barbarians had not left, intact under the conflagration, such material testimony of her passage through history as the kings with the masks of gold. The Phoenicians desert the coast of the Peloponnesus, of Attica, and of Crete, and the native populations, dispersed like a city of bees on which a host of wasps has descended, swarm in every direction, on the shores of Asia, in Sicily, and in southern Italy. Silence reigns around continental Greece. It was to be two or three hundred years before the Phoenicians and the Achaeans, driven away by the invasion, could get back the route to its gulfs.

Bust of Pericles, ▶
Roman copy of a Greek original,
c. 425 B.C.
British Museum, London.

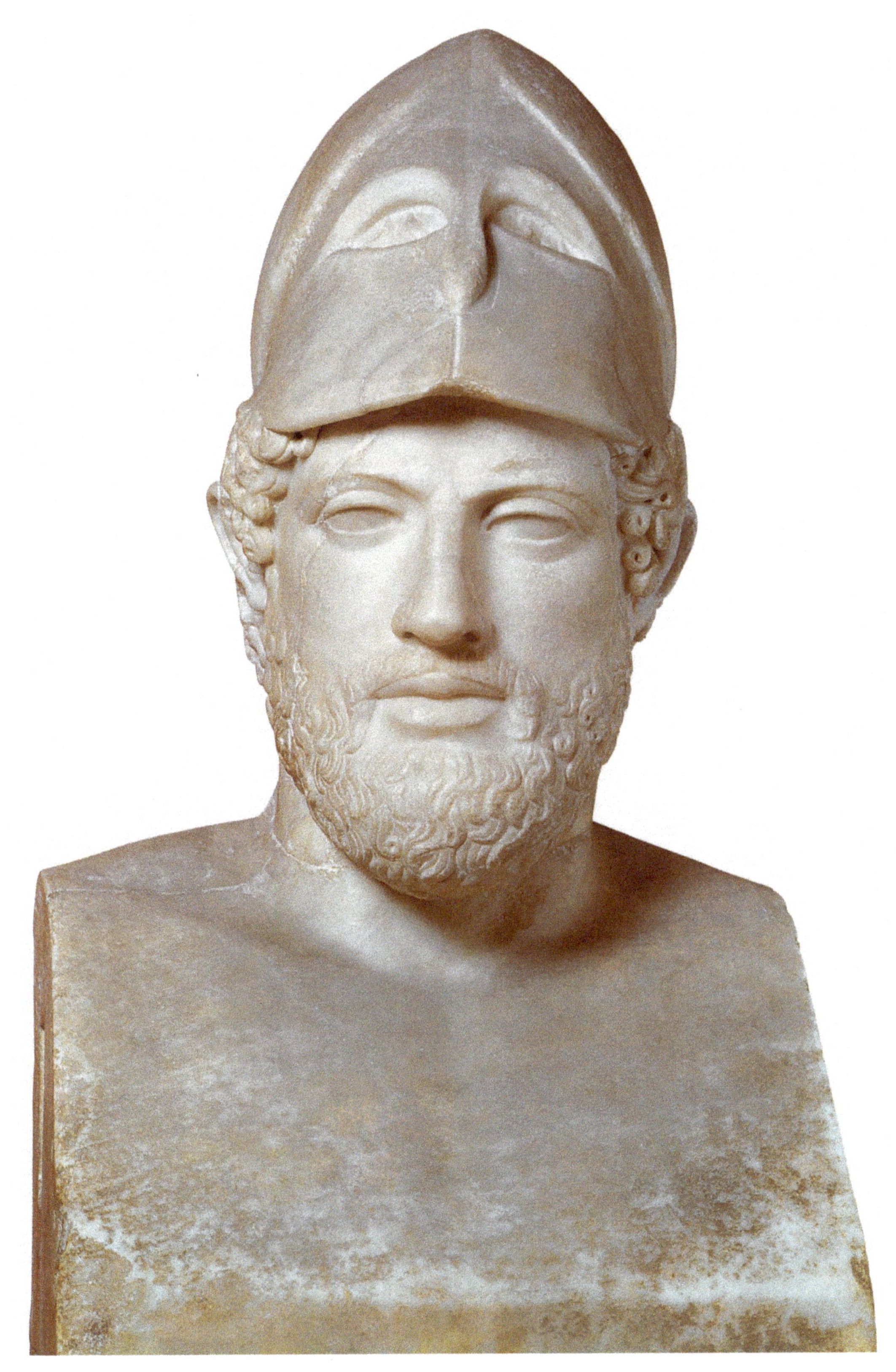

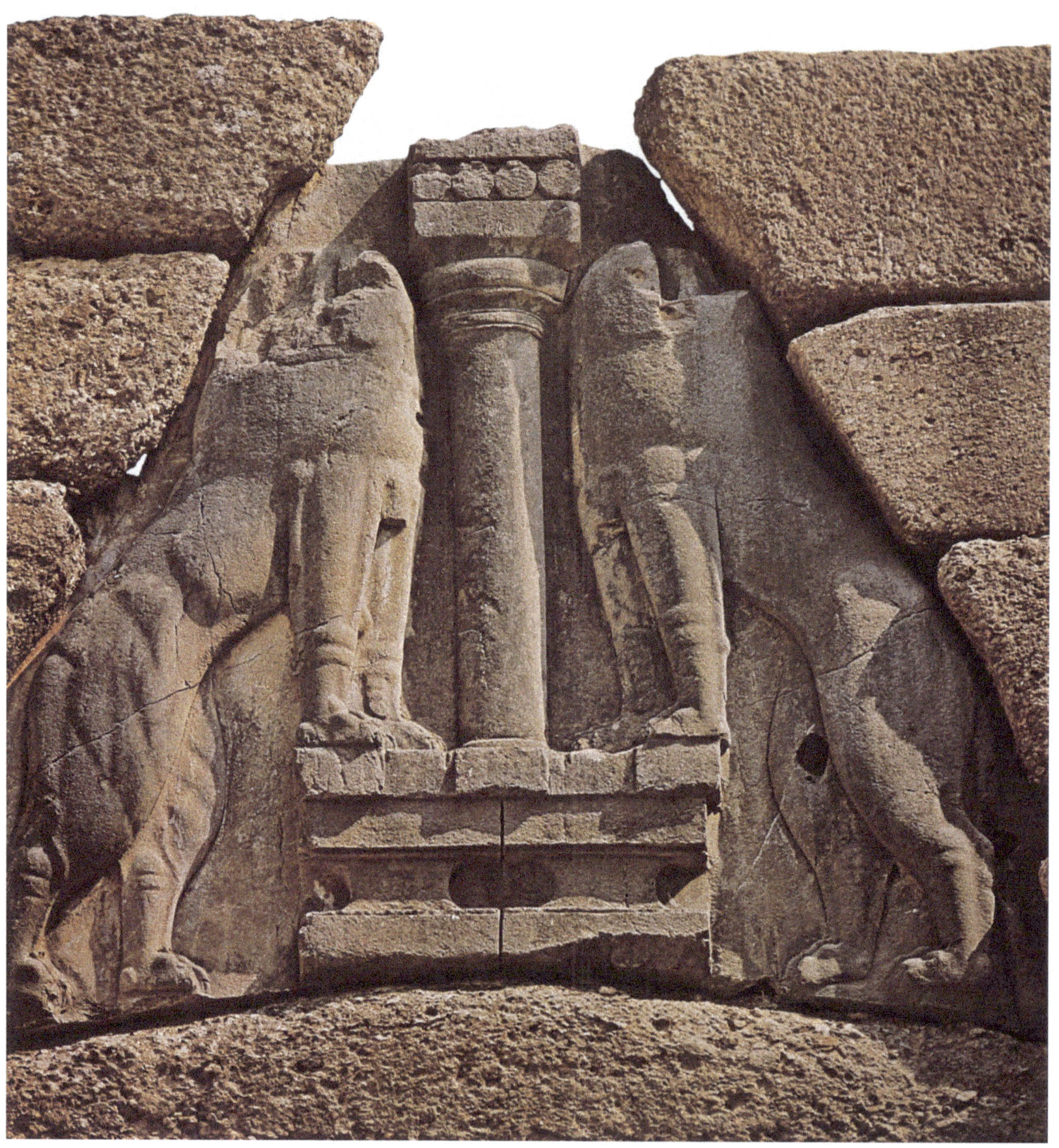

THE SOURCES OF GREEK ART

The Dorians had no word to say during the Hellenic Middle Ages; nothing from Asia entered their land. The ancient continent was advancing step by step, by way of the islands, prudently regaining a little of the lost territory. Melos, in need of pottery, had to wait till the Ceramists of primitive Athens had manufactured at the Dipylon (workshop of an ancient Greek vase painter, active around 760–750 BC), those vases with the geometrical designs which were the first sign of the reawakening witnessing a slow dramatic ascent in the shadows of the soul, under this magnificent sky, at the center of this brilliant world. In order that the spark might kindle, it was necessary that the Dorian, the Phoenician, and the ancient Aegean who has become an Ionian, repair their broken relationships. Thereupon the flame mounted quicker to light up the virgin soil with the most dazzling focus of intelligence in history.

For this focus, the Homeric poems — echoes picked up from the annihilated world by the vanquished — and the radiant Greek myths which are elaborated confusedly along the deserted shores are the heralding dawn lights seen against this black background. The cradle of the Hellenic soul mounts with them on the chariot of the sun.

In the evening, the Dorian herdsman bringing home his goats from the mountain and the Ionian sailor bringing home his bark from the sea would repeat to themselves glorious fables which carried over into images men's old intuitive notions of the phenomena of nature, or translated the struggle of their ancestors against the adverse forces of the ill-organized world. The enthusiastic naturism of the human soul in its freshness gave to its young science a robe of light, of clouds, of leaves, and of waters. The whole religion, the philosophy, the austere and charming soul of the builders of the Parthenon are in this anonymous and tangled poem which rises with the murmur of a dawn as Greece reawakens to life.

The "Greek miracle" was necessary. The whole ancient world had prepared, had willed its coming. During the fruitful silence when the Dorians were "accumulating within themselves the strength of their soil, Egypt and Assyria

◀ **The Lion Gate at Mycenae,**
the only known monumental sculpture of Bronze Age Greece XIV century B.C.
In situ.

kept their lead. But they were discouraged and stricken by the cold of age. They were to become the initiators of the Hellenic Renaissance, as they had been the guides for the childhood of the peoples of the Archipelago.

The Greeks had the privilege of inhabiting a land so inundated, steeped and saturated with light, so clearly defined by its own structure, that the eyes of man had only to open, to draw from it its law. When man enters a bay closed in by an amphitheater of mountains between an illuminated sky and water that rolls rays of light, as if a spring of flame welled up under its waves, he is at the center of a slightly dark sapphire set in a circle of gold. The masses and the lines organize themselves so simply, cutting such clear profiles on the limpidity of space that their essential relations spontaneously impress themselves on the mind. There is not a country in the world which addresses itself to the intelligence with more insistence, force, and precision than this one. All the typical aspects of the universe offer themselves, with the earth — everywhere penetrated by the sea, with the horizon of the sea, the bony islands, the straits, golden and mauve between two liquid masses glittering even in the heart of the night, the rocks repeating from morning to evening all the changes of space and the sun, with the dark forests on the mountains, with the pale forests in the valleys, with the hills everywhere surrounding the dry plains, and — bordered by pink laurel — the streams, whose whole course one can embrace at a glance.

Life in this land keeps close to its earth, is active without excess, and simple. Neither misery nor wealth nor poverty. Houses are of wood, clothing of skins, and there is the cold water of the torrents to wash off the dust and blood of the stadium. There is not much meat, that of the goat which grazes among the fissures of the rocks, perhaps, but there is a little wine mixed with resin and honey and kept in skins; there are milk, bread, the fruits of the dry countries, the orange, the fig, and the olive. There is nothing on the horizon or in social life which could give birth to or develop mystic tendencies. A nature religion exists, a very rough one — in the beliefs of the people, perhaps even rather coarse, but welling up from springs so pure and so poetized by the singers that when the philosophers think to oppose it they do no more than extract from it the rational conception of the world barely hidden in its symbols. Doubtless man fears the gods.

But since the gods resemble him, they do not turn his life from the normal and natural relationships which bind it with that of other men. The priest has but little influence. Greece is perhaps the only one of the old countries where the priest did not live outside the pale of popular life in order to represent to the people the great mysteries as a world apart. Hence the rapidity of this people's evolution and the freedom of its investigations.

Bull-leaping fresco, ▶
62,3 cm, 1700-1400 B.C.
Archeological Museum of Heraklion, Crete.

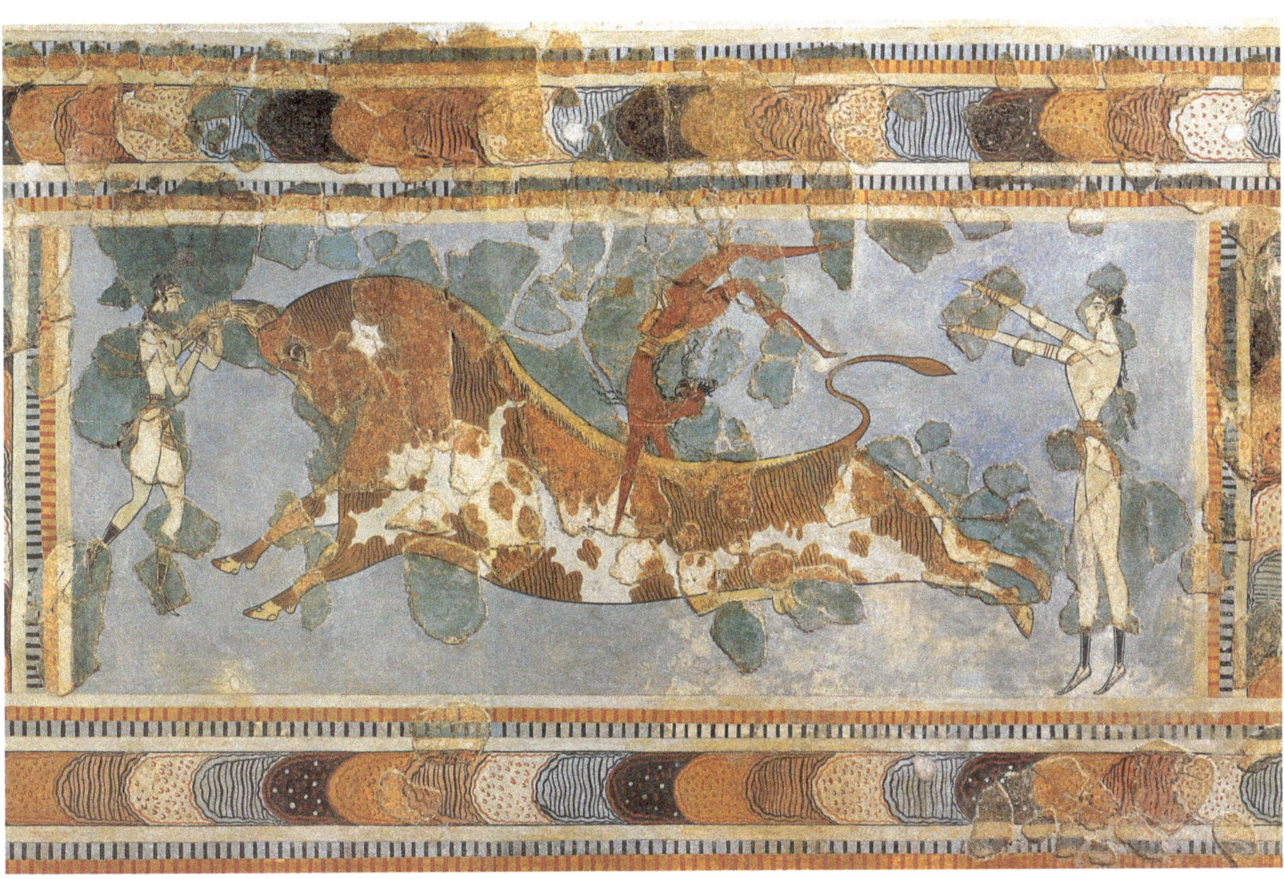

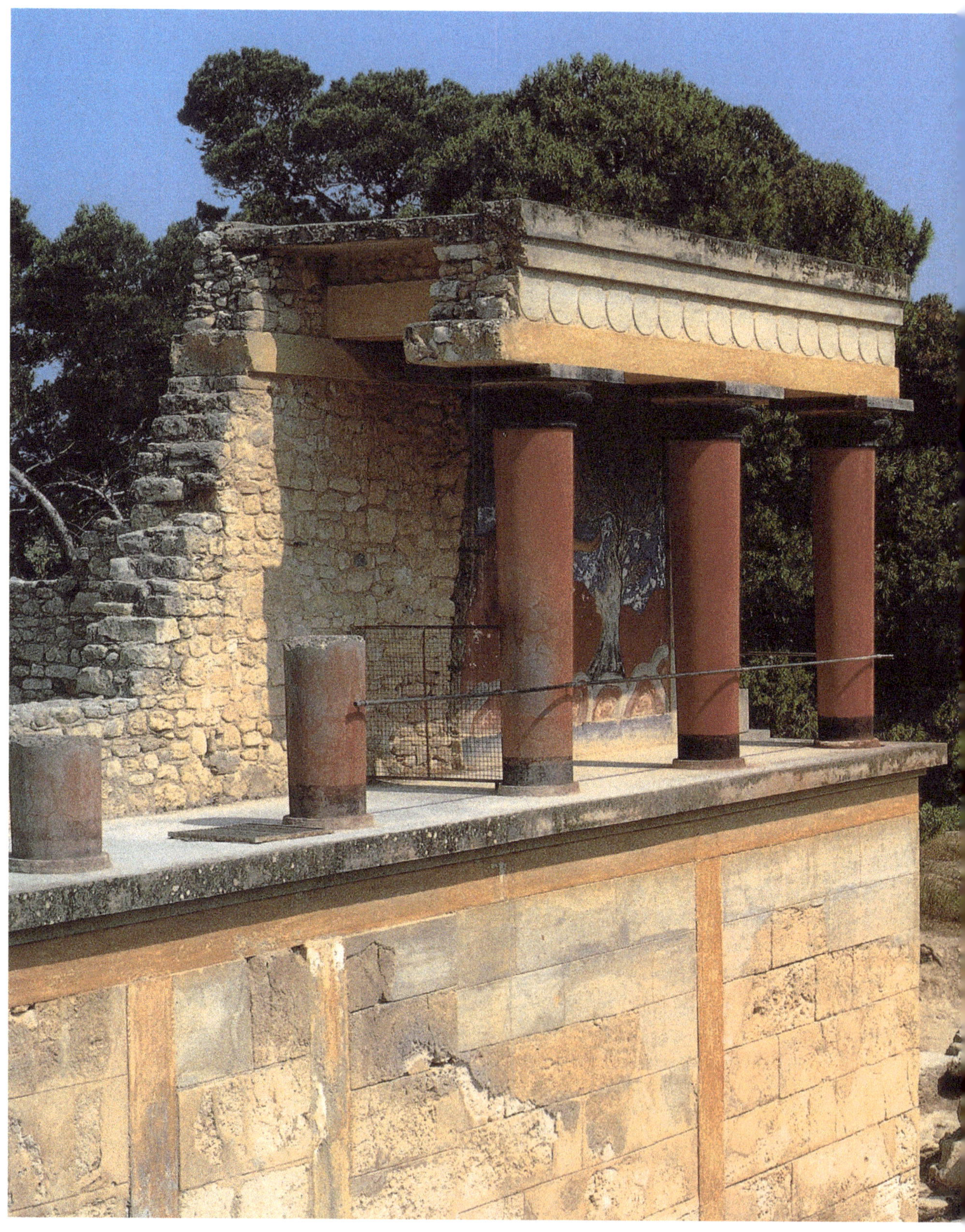

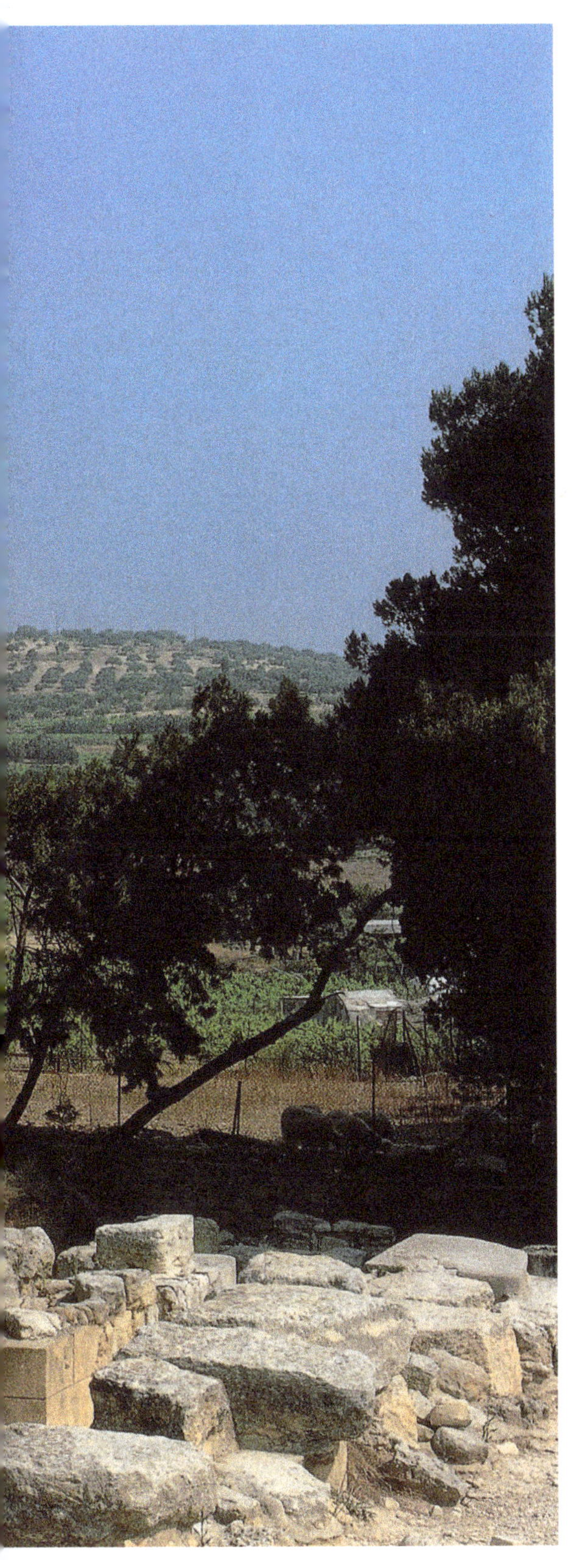

THE DORIANS

Although man already places himself under the protection of the intelligent forces, he has not forgotten the struggles which his ancestor was forced to maintain against the brutal forces of a universe which repulsed him. This memory is inscribed in the sculptures which, on the pediment of the Parthenon of Peisistratus (ruler of ancient Athens between c. 561 and 527 B. C.), showed Zeus struggling against Typhon (monstrous snaky giant), or Herakles (son of Zeus) throwing Echidna (a monster, half-woman and half-snake) to earth. A barbarous work, violently painted with blues, greens, and reds, a memory of avalanches, of terrifying caverns, of the storms of the north, it was a nightmare of savages still ill taught by Asia and Egypt, but becoming curious and already eager to comprehend. The hell of the pagans will last but a short time.

◀ **Palace of Knossos**, Crete
1700-1400 B.C.

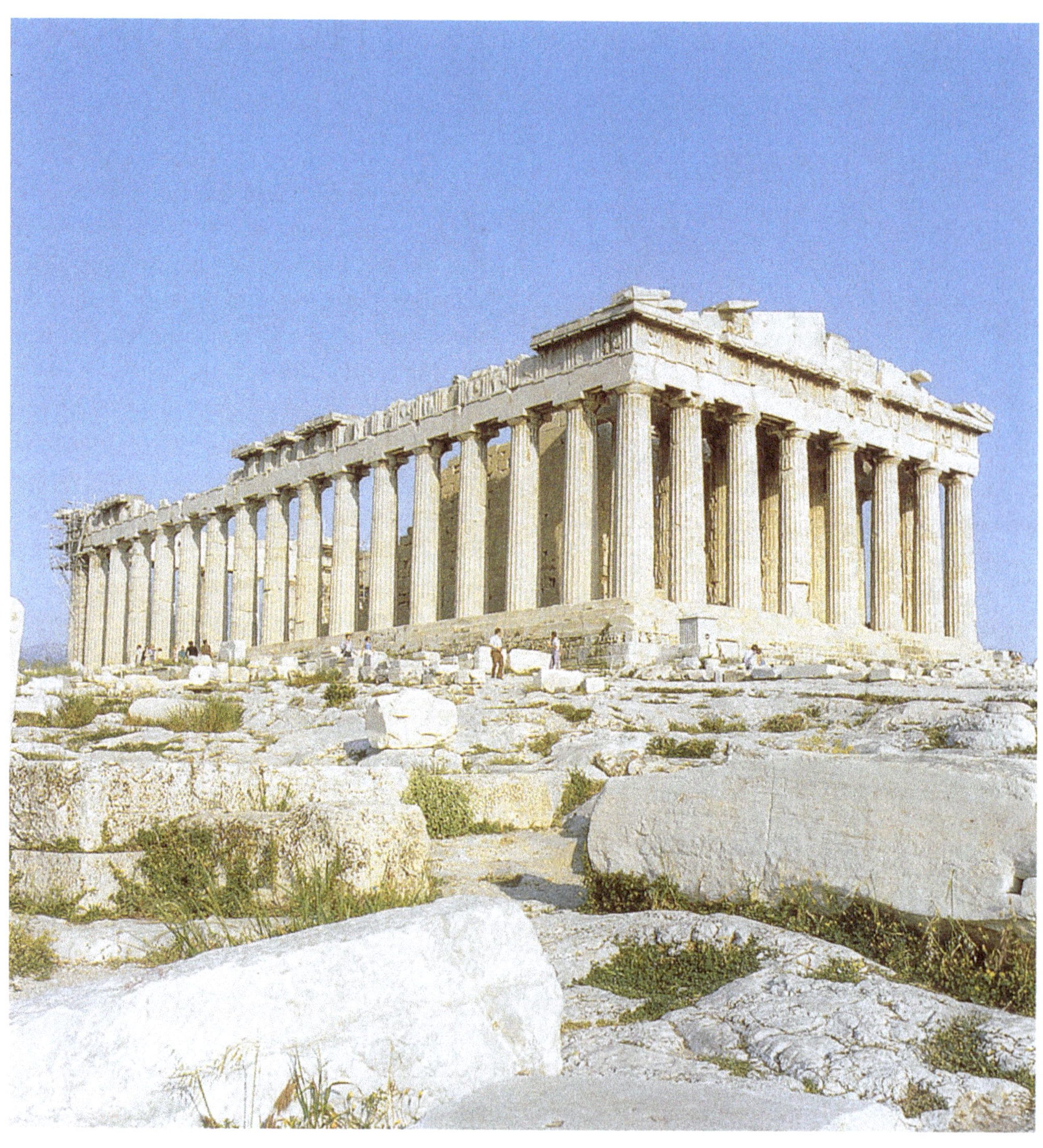

DORIAN ART AND ARCHITECTURE

The temple where these idols reign, these bulls, these twisted serpents, these astonished visages with green beards, is, moreover, in its principle, what it will be in the greatest periods. Architecture is the collective, necessary art which appears first and dies first. The primordial desire of man, after food, is shelter, and it is in order to erect that shelter that, for the first time, he appeals to his faculty of discovering in natural constructions a certain logic permitting him to organize his life according to the plan of the universe. The forest and the cliffs are the powerful educators in the geometrical abstraction from which man is to draw the means of building houses which are to have a chance of resisting the assault of rain and storms. At Corinth there already raises a temple with heavy and very broad columns, coming straight up from the ground as they mount in a block to the entablature. Several of them still stand. They are terrible to see, black, gnawed like old trees, as hard as the mind of the Peloponnesian countries. The Doric order

◀ Parthenon
Temple
447-432-B.C.
Athens

came from those peasant houses which one still sees in the countryside of Asia Minor, trees set in the ground in four lines making a rectangle, supporting other trees on which the roof was to be placed. The form of the pediment comes from the slope of this roof, which is designed to carry off the rain. The Greek temple, even when it realizes the most lucid and the most consciously willed intellectual combinations, sends its roots into the world of matter, of which it is the formulated law.

On the sculptures of these temples the mind of Asia has left its trace. They are continued until the great century, but so assimilated in the nascent Hellenic genius that on seeing them one cannot think of direct imitation, but rather of those uncertain and fleeting resemblances which hover on the face of children. The archaic Dorian Apollos (God of music, poetry, art, oracles, archery, plague, medicine, sun, light and knowledge), those smiling and terrible statues through which force mounts like a flood, make one think of the Egyptian forms, because of the leg which steps forward and the arms glued to the stiff torso. But on this hieratism the theocratic spirit exercises no action. Dorian art is all of a piece, far less subtle, far less refined, far less conscious than that of the sculptors of Thebes. The passages between the very brusque sculptural planes are scarcely indicated. What dominates is the need to express the life of the muscles.

It is because these Apollos are athletes. The great cult of gymnastics is born, that necessary institution which is to permit Greece to develop the strength of arms and of legs, while parallel with it there develops suppleness of the mind in its constant search for the universal equilibrium. Already, from all the regions of the Greek world, from the islands, from the distant colonies, from Italy and from Asia, the young men come to Olympia and Delphi to contest the crown of olive leaves. In running, in wrestling, and in throwing the discus they are nude. The artists, who hasten to these national meeting places, like everyone else who calls himself a Hellene, have before their eyes the spectacle of the movements of the human frame and of the complex play of the muscles rolling under the brown skin, which shows them as if they were bare themselves, and which is hardened by scars, Greek sculpture is born in the stadium.

It was to take a century to climb the steps of the stadium and to install itself in the pediments of the final Parthenon, where it was to become the educator of the poets and, after them, of the philosophers. They were to feast their mind on the spectacle of the increasingly subtle relationships which sculpture established in the world of forms in action. There was never a more glorious or more striking example of the unity of our activity: athleticism, by the intermediary

of sculpture, is the father of philosophy, at least, of Platonian philosophy (Plato 428/427 or 424/423 – 348/347 BC), whose first concern was to turn against sculpture and athleticism in order to kill them.

Through the Dorian Apollo Greece passes from primitive art to archaism, properly so-called. The artist considers the form with more attention, painstakingly disengages the meaning of it, and transports that meaning to his work in so uncompromising a manner that he imposes on it the appearance of an edifice, whose architectonic quality seems destined to know no change. The Peloponnesus becomes the great training school of the archaic marble workers; c, Aristocles (1st century AD), Canachus (latter part of the 6th century BCE), and Hagelaides open workshops at Argos, Sicyon, and Sparta; the citadel of the Dorian ideal becomes, before Athens, the focus of Greek thought. But Hellenism in its entirety is not to find its nourishment there. Sparta is far from the routes of the Old World, imprisoned in a solitary valley where mountain torrents flow; it is a fertile but a jealous country, separated from the great horizons by the hard ridges of the Taygetus (mountain range in the Peloponnese peninsula), which are covered with snow even in summer. The people which dwells there is as closed as the valley itself.

Temple of Hephaestus ▶
449-415 B.C.
Athens

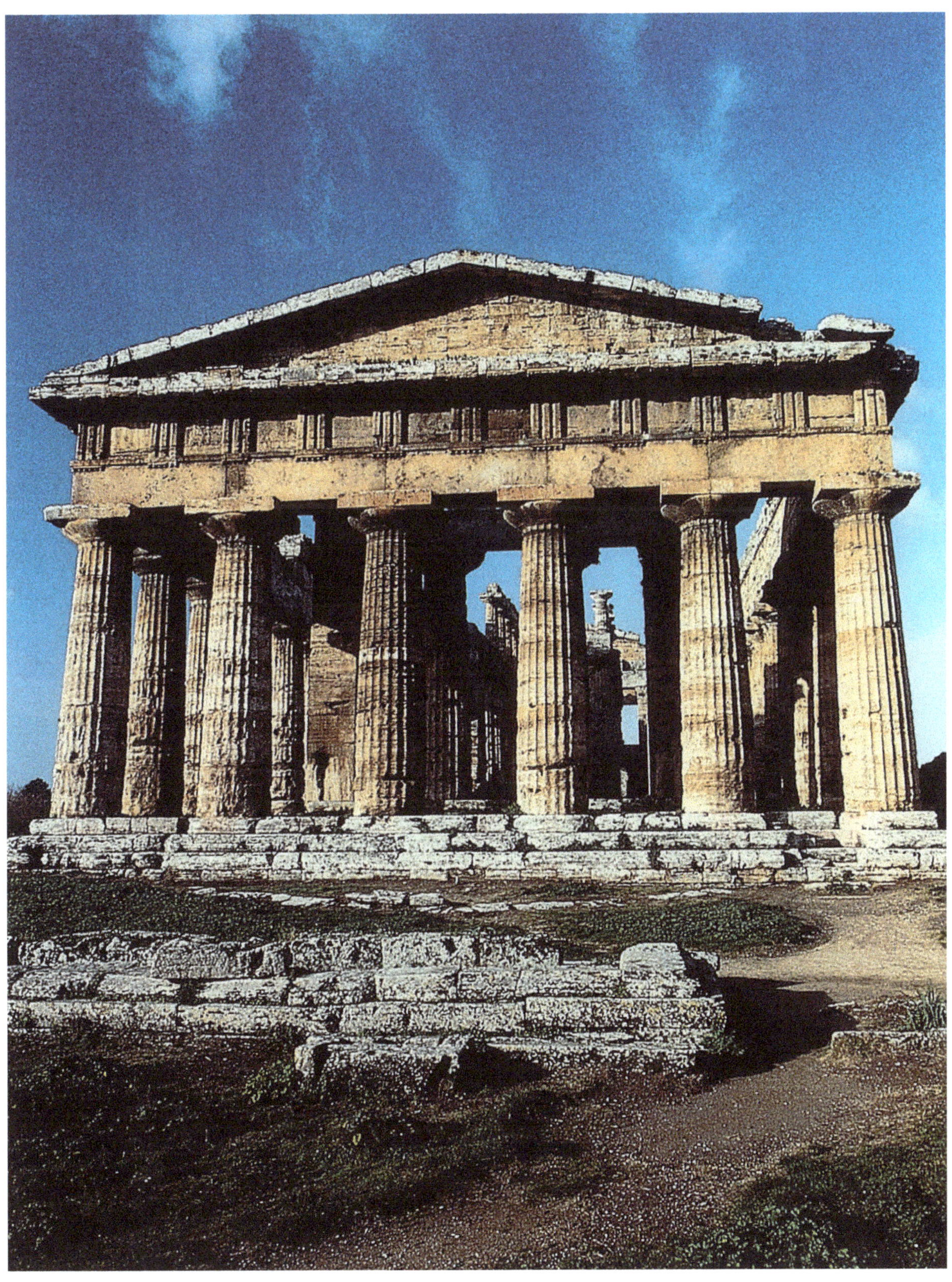

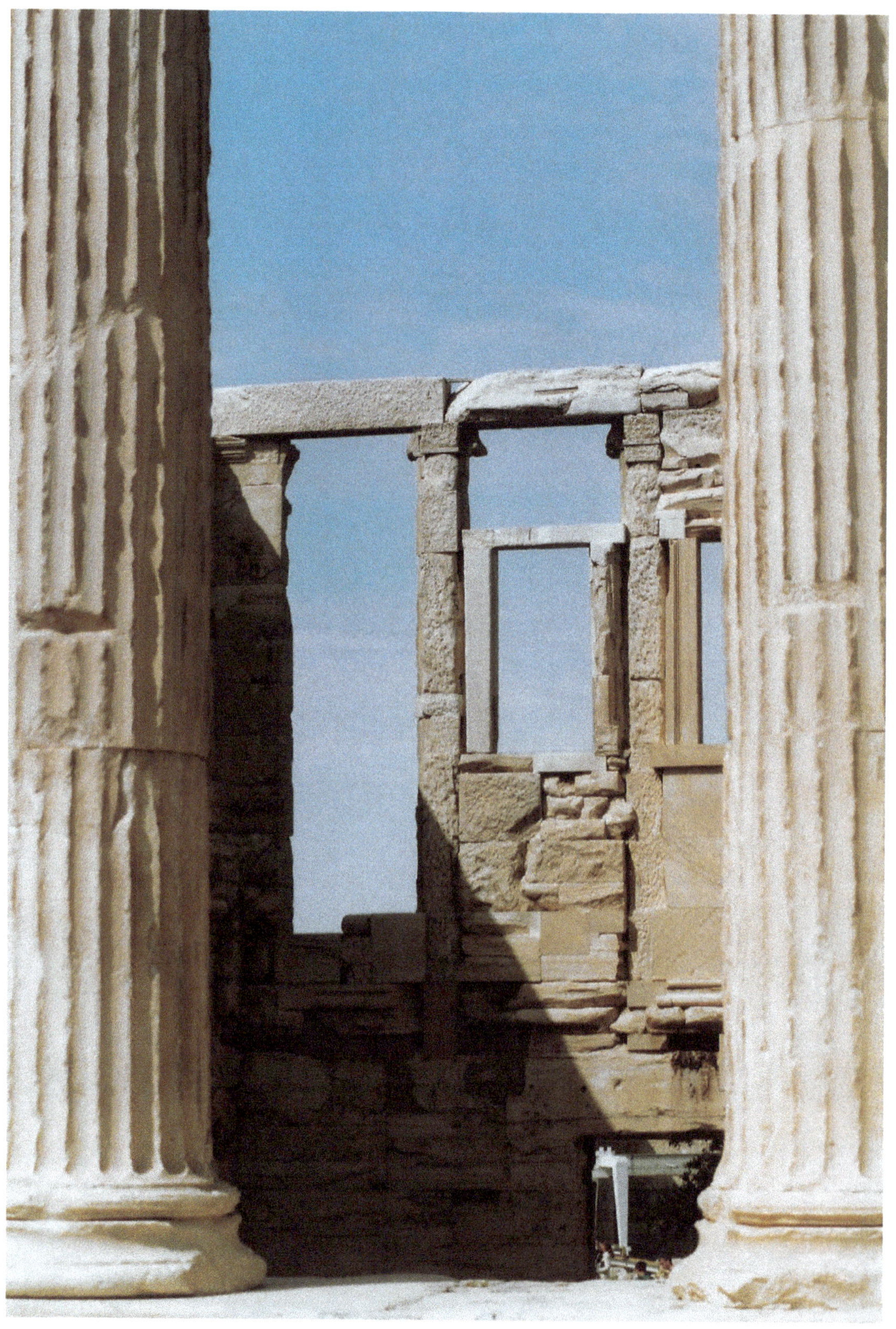

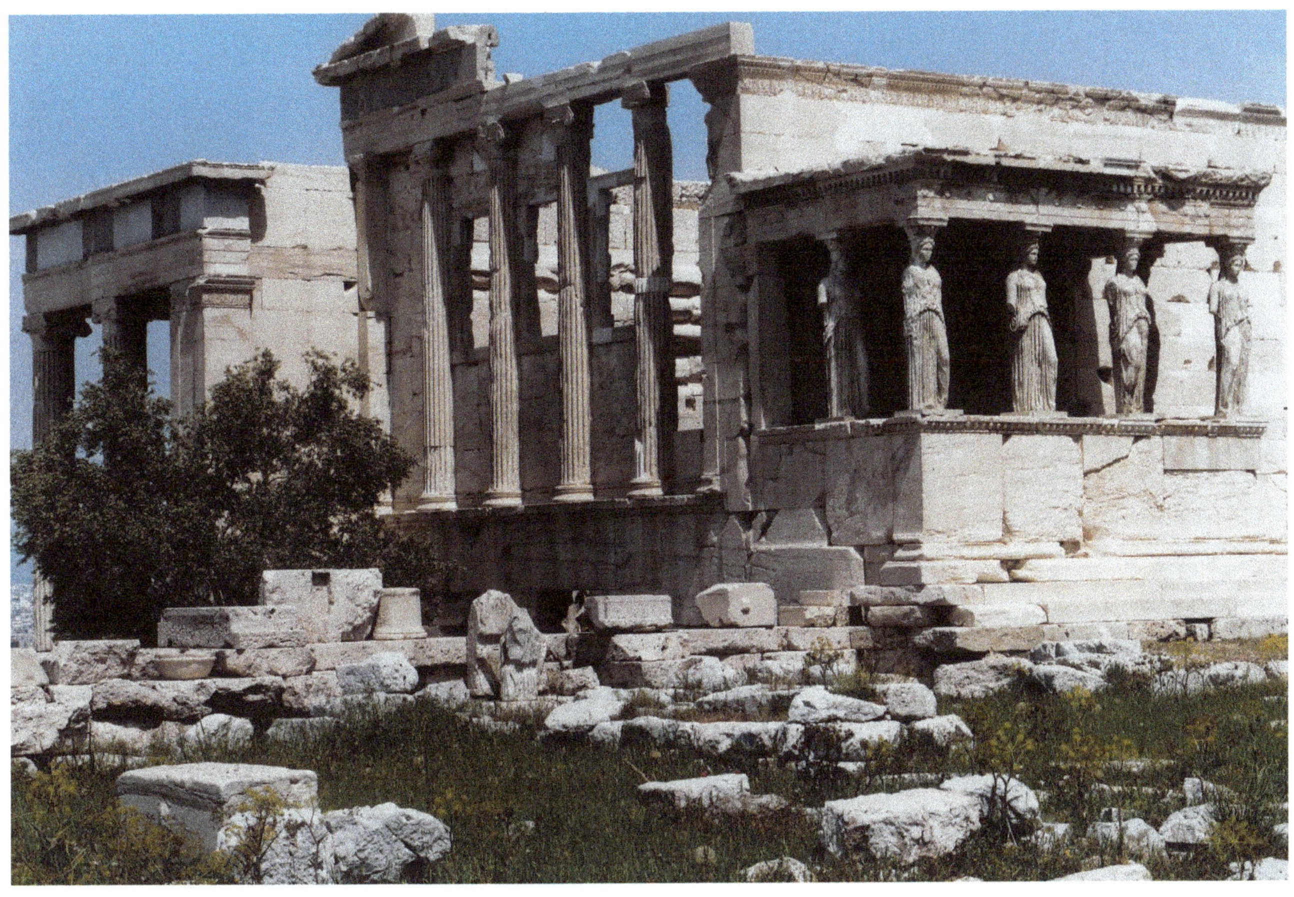

◀ Erechtheum
421-406 B.C.

▲ View of the rear façade of the Erechtheum

Athens, on the contrary, is at the center of the eastern Mediterranean, and near the sea. It is the meeting point of the positive and disciplined Dorian element, which mounts from the south toward Corinth, Aegina, and Attica in its search for lands to dominate, and of the Ionian element which brings to the city, through the sieve of the islands, the artist spirit of Asia, made supple and subtle by the habits of trade, diplomacy and smuggling. The glory of Sparta, in reality, is that of having offered to Athens a virgin soil to fertilize and also, by harassing her without mercy, to have kept her in condition, to have compelled her for a long time to cultivate her energy. Athens, tempered by these struggles, was not slow in showing her superiority. When the soldiers of Darius (c. 550–486 BCE) followed the traders of Asia to the European coast, it is she who was at the head of the Greeks, while Sparta, enclosed in the blind cult of her personal interest, took her place only after the combat.

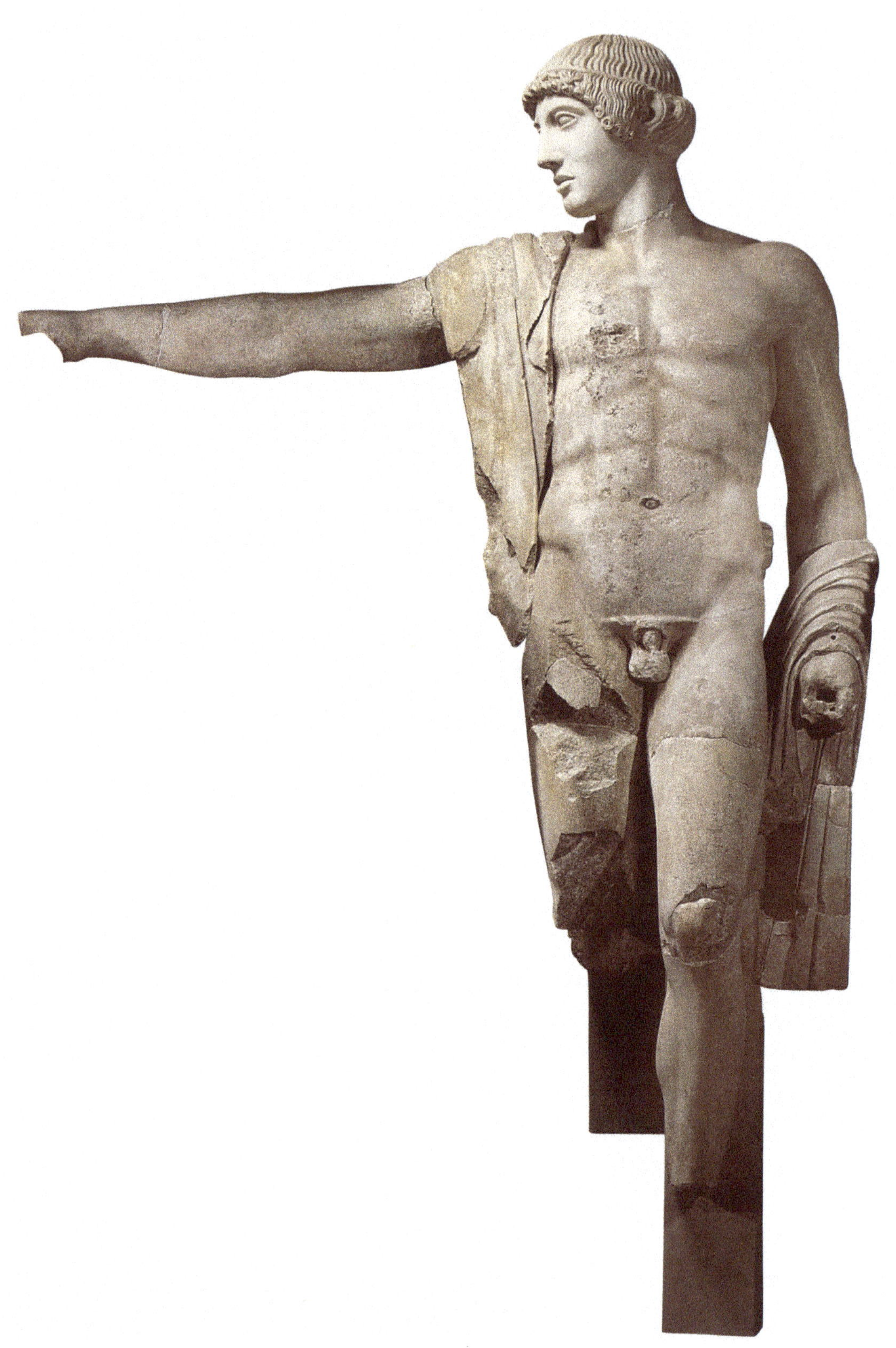

THE HERA OF SAMOS

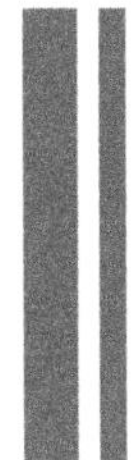

Where are we to find the first step of Ionian art in its march toward Attica - the uncertain dawn of the great oriental sensualism rendered healthy by the sea and sharpened by commerce, which will flood the Dorian soul with humanity? The Hera of Samos is, perhaps, even stiffer than the Peloponnesian athletes, as it is nearer to the Saite Period (664–525 BC), which is unfolding at this moment and investing hieratic form with a humanity of its own. A tight sheath of cloth imprisons the legs, which are close together, but under the figure's light veil, with its lines like those on water, the shoulders, the arms, the breast, and the hollowed back have profiles of a moving grace, and planes which meet one another and interpenetrate with the delicacy of a confession. It is this spirit of abounding tenderness which is soon to take root on the Greek continent. From the end of the sixth century Dorian art and Ionian art were neighbors everywhere without having yet recognized each other fully. At Delphi, at the threshold of the Treasury of the Cnidians (ancient Greek city of Caria), Asiatic Greece saluted with a mysterious smile the rude statue maker of the Peloponnesus who had set up the women, the lions, and the formidable horses in the pediment of the Sanctuary of Apollo. The caryatids (female figure serving as an architectural support) which supported the Asiatic architrave were strange, secret women; they had a winged grace, like that of an animal and of a dance; they seemed to guard the gate of temptation, which led to a warmth within, like that of the sun. The Dorian spirit and the Ionian spirit — the young countryman bursting with vigor and the woman bedecked, caressing, questionable — met and loved. Attic art, which in its adult age was to be the great classic sculpture, austere and living, was to be born of their union.

◄ **Apollon,**
Temple of Zeus, Olympia,
c. 470-456 B.C., Marble, h : 330 cm
Archeological Museum, Olympia

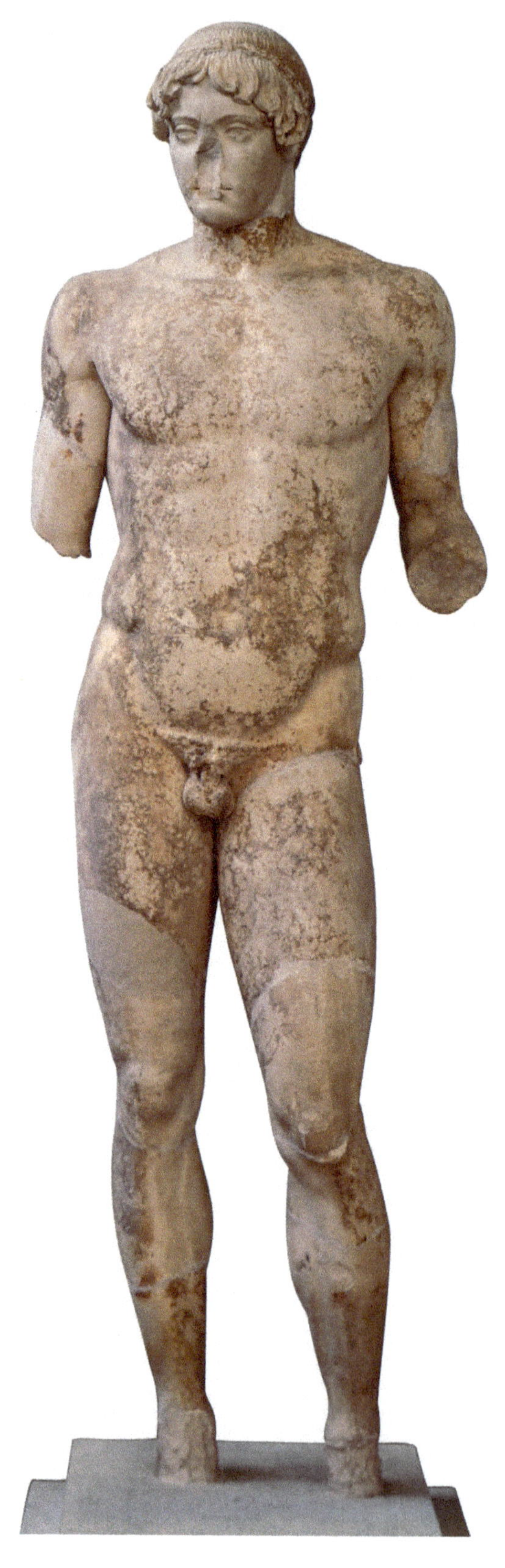

THE IONIANS

arble had been skillfully treated in Athens for more than a hundred years, and the Acropolis, especially at the time of Peisistratus (561-527 BC), had been covered with monuments and statues. But Endoios (middle of the 6th century BC), the great Athenian master of the sixth century, still remained subject to Ionian traditions. It was only on the eve of the Median wars (499-449 BC) that the Hellenic synthesis, before manifesting itself by the collective action of resistance to the invader, is outlined in certain minds. Undoubtedly, a people is too complex an organism, and one whose generating elements merge too closely and are too numerous to permit us to determine the degree of influence of each one of these elements in all the acts which express the people. It is like a river made up of a hundred streams, of a thousand torrents or brooks which bring to it, mixed together. The men of this time are united to those who precede them and to those who follow them by necessary relationships wherein the mysterious continuity of our activity is manifested. It is not possible to fix the moment or to designate the work in which the Hellenic soul, as we call it today, tried to define itself for the first time. We can only turn our eyes to those works which possess the first quiver of life, over which there seems to pass the first breath of liberty and spiritual joy, in order that we may surprise in them the awakening of a new humanity to the beauty of living.

The young women found near the Erechtheion, amid the rubbish of the foundations of the Parthenon, where the Greek workmen had put them after the sacking and burning of the Acropolis by the soldiers of Xerxes (c. 518–465 BC), were, perhaps, the first who had the smile of intoxication which announces the awakening. Undoubtedly the perfume of the islands was predominant with them. They think above all of pleasing; they are feminine. But on seeing the surety of their planes and their definite and powerful equilibrium, we cannot doubt that the Dorian artisan, who was then working at Aegina, Corinth, and even Athens, had repeated contact with the Ionian immigrant whom the Persian conquest had driven back to the Occident.

◀ Apollo of Omphalos Theater of Dionysus Eleuthereus, Athens Replica of the Greek original, c. 460 B.C.
Marbel, h: 176 cm.
National Archeological Museum, Athens

Brought from the Orient by the adventurers of the sea, these women take good care not to shock the hard, austere world which they have come to visit. They remain motionless, holding up their robes with one hand. Their red hair, which hangs on their backs and whose tresses fall on each side of their necks to rest on their breasts, is plaited and curled; it is dyed, doubtless, and streams with jewels. Sometimes their foreheads are diademed, their wrists encircled with bracelets, their ears loaded with rings. From head to foot they are painted, with blue, red, ocher, and yellow, and their eyes of enamel glow in their smiling faces. These creatures so barbarously illuminated, dazzling and bizarre as the birds of the tropics, have the strong savor of the painted and adorned women of the Orient; they are somewhat vulgar, perhaps, but fascinating nonetheless, like things from afar off, like fairy-tale beings. They are beautiful. We love them with a tenderness which cannot exhaust itself.

They have overturned the curious notions that were anchored in us by academic idealism. For three hundred years it regarded immaculate marble as a sentimental emblem of serenity — one which never existed, except in the minds of certain philosophers, at the hour when Greece was approaching her decline. And white marble also stood for a perfection which, it is to be hoped, we shall not attain — discontent, curiosity, and effort being the very condition of life. Until the complete unfolding of her art in any case, and probably until her fall, Greece painted her gods and her temples. Variegated with blues and reds, alive like men and women, the gods became animated at break of day, took part in the surprises and joys of the light, and moved in the depth of the gathering shadow. They belonged to the crowd that swarmed at the foot of the Acropolis, the busy, noisy, familiar crowd of a port leading to the Orient; they came out of the dirty alleys where stray dogs fought for scraps of offal. We see them pass before the shop windows where the port spreads out its quarters of mutton and lamb, its fruits, its heaps of spices, its dyed stuffs, and its glassware; they are in the colorful squares so full of cries and calls — of the odors of garlic, rotting food, and aromatic herbs. We see the women with the painted eyes, dressed in their garish clothing.

The temples and the monuments covered with ocher, with vermilion, green, azure, and gold, are made up of the tones of the sky, of the space over the sea — greenish or flushed with purple, they have the colors of the sea, violet or blue, of the earth, of its dress of thin crops and dry foliage, with the milky olive trees and the black cypresses as they marry their forms to the ever-present forms, of the sinuous bays and the hills. What is the role of the statue maker? It is to balance, in the lucidity and the firmness of his intelligence, all these scattered elements, so that on their apparent chaos he may impose clear relationships and harmonious directions.

The Riace Bronze B, ▶
Bronze Sculptures
460-450 B.C., h: 197
Museo Nazionale, Reggio Calabria.

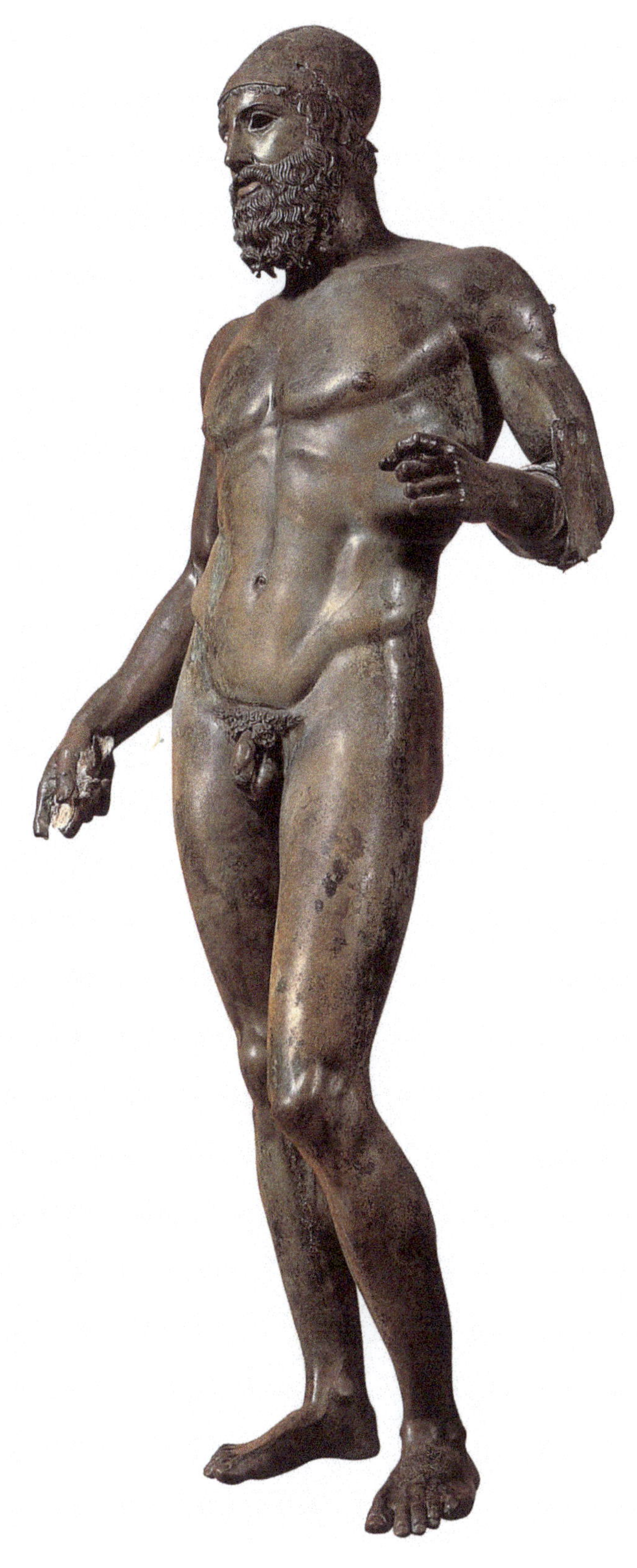

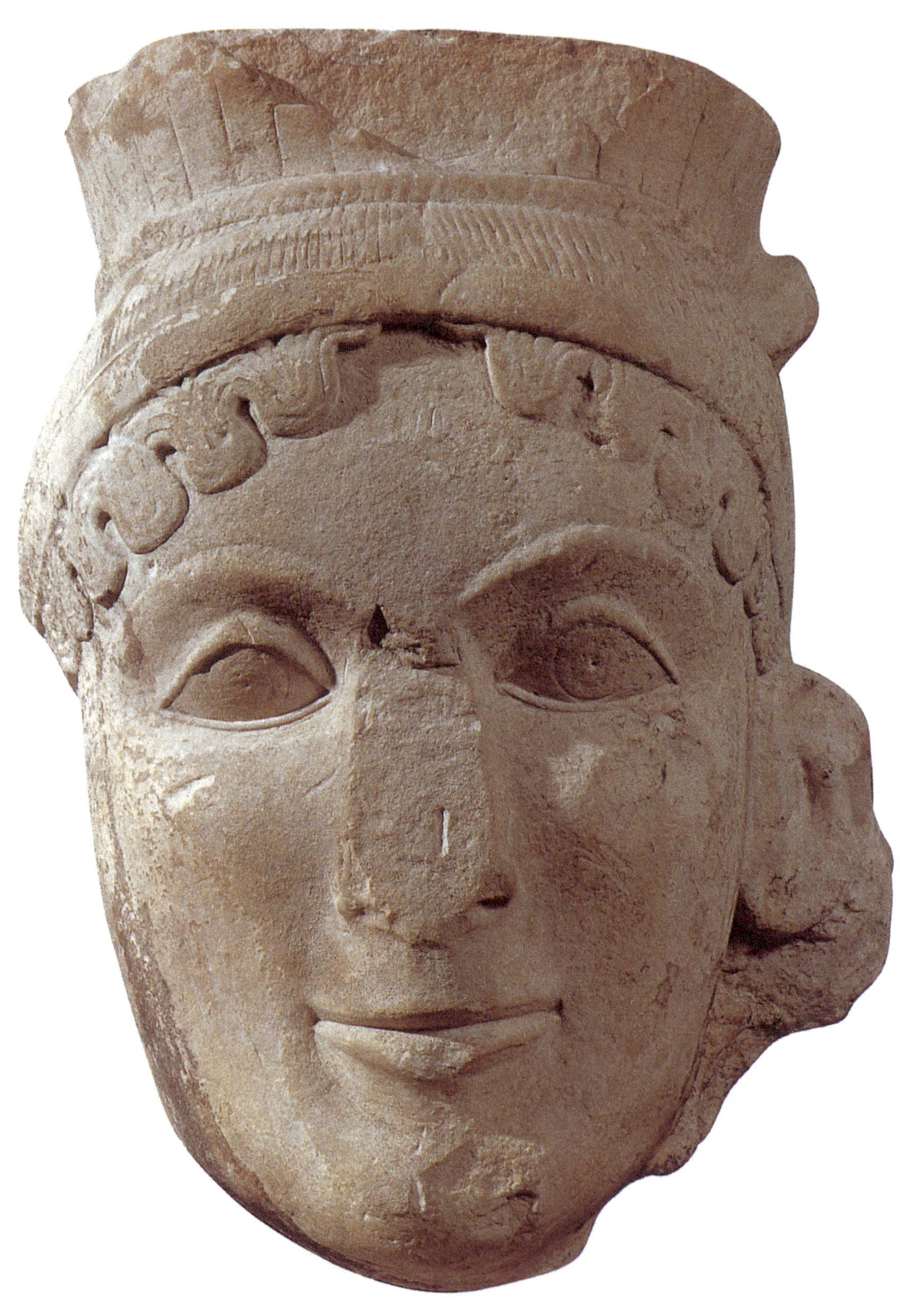

THE APOLLONIAN MYTH

The Apollonian myth kept watch in the consciousness — obscure as yet, but solid and swelling with primitive faith — of the Athenian marble cutters. The strange women who had taken possession of the Athenian fortress could not have unnerved for more anthropomorphist which they had preceded by only a short time. Already the element of orgies and sentimental excess represented by their polychromy had been held in check at every point by clear-cut planes and precise contours, thereby sustaining its alluring, smiling action. The miraculous and fatigued soul of Asia recovers its strength and its faith upon contact with this fierce energy, which it enlightens with intelligence in an unexpected exchange. We have reached the mysterious hour when the flower will unfold to the light the tremble of its petals, which till now had been pressed together in their green sheath. These idols represent, perhaps, man's finest effort to discover in his consciousness the approbation of his instinct. There is in them a tension of soul which moves us, an energy devoted wholly to searching out our agreement of an hour with a world whose secret harmony we feel to live within us. Ingenuous as youth, perverse as desire, they are as firm and as free as the will.

With them Greek archaism possessed itself completely of that architectural conception of form which may be very dangerous because it carries with it the risk of never escaping from it, as in the case of the Egyptians. It is admirable. It is necessary. It is a more elevated form in the eyes of some than the balanced expression of our earthly destiny which the fifth century was to realize among the Greeks. And it is to forget, indeed, that the art of the fifth century, even when it broke the frames of archaic form to let the palpitation and the atmosphere of life enter them by torrents, retained all the principles which make the strength and the austerity of that form.

◀ **Hera The Temple of Hera,**
Olympia, c. 600 B.C
Limestone, h: 52 cm.
Archeological Museum, Olympia

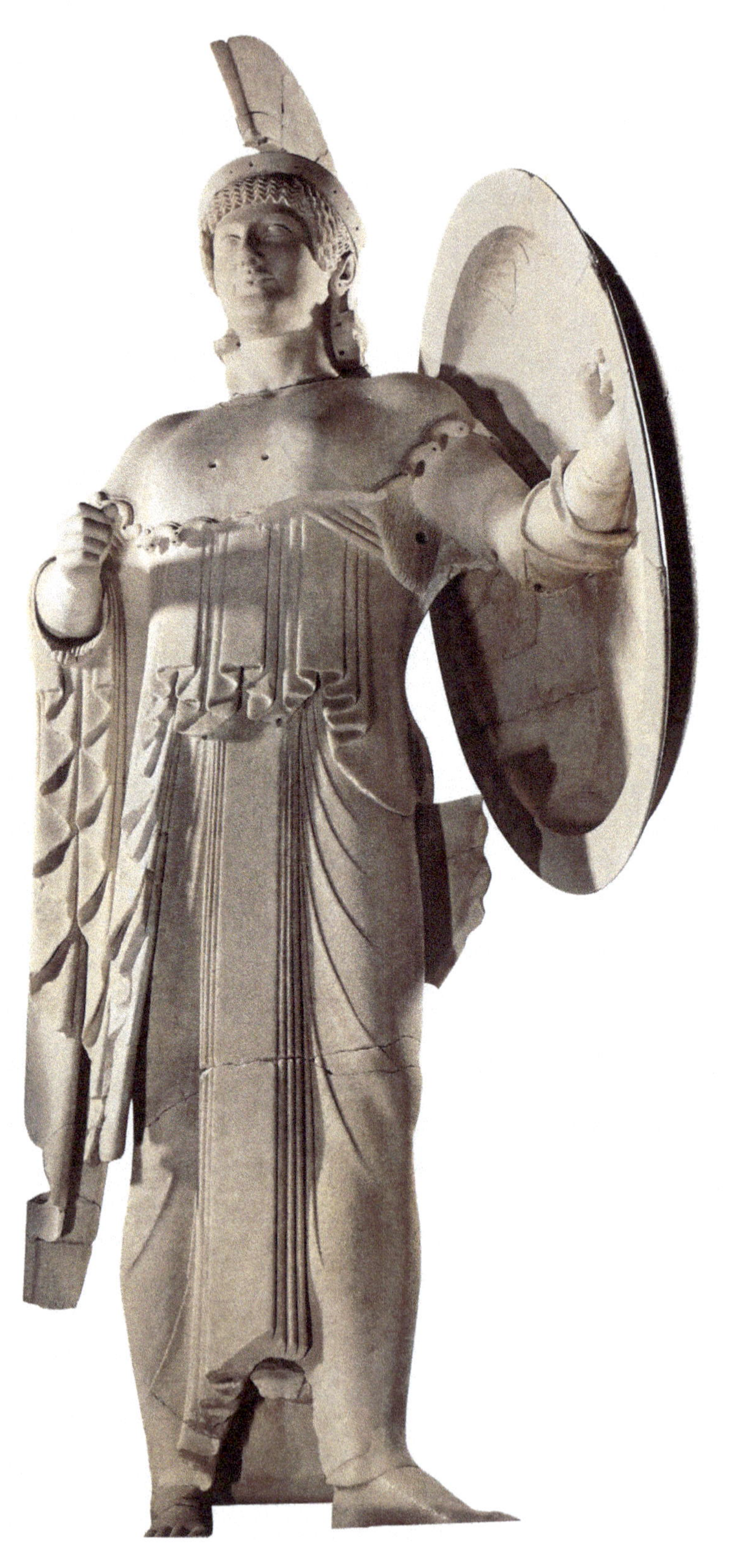

THE HELLENISTIC PERIOD

Until the Hellenistic period the radiance of Greece in the Mediterranean world prevented men from perceiving the civilizations which were growing up or disappearing round about her. The nation she knew best and of which she spoke most favorably was Persia, because it was the power she had to combat. The old peoples had hardly more than one means of intermingling with and comprehending one another, which was war. Now, military conquest was repugnant to the Greeks. The colonies which they had sown on all the shores of Asia, the Euxine, North Africa, southern Italy, and Sicily constituted a network of stations in their vast maritime system which was pretty closely reserved for the nation, and beyond which everything, for them, was legends, semi-darkness, and confusion. Trade scarcely got beyond the coasts of the happy seas. The interior of the lands, the mountains of the horizon, the unknown forests, withheld their secret from Greece, since they escaped her influence.

Hellenism has left only furtive traces outside of the Greek world, properly so-called. There was, perhaps, only one agricultural and non-maritime people that was strongly influenced by Greece, through the cities of Magna Graecia and through the sea routes. The country that lies between the Arno, the Tiber, the Apennines, and the sea was probably the only one of the old world to accept, without resistance, and from the heroic period onward, the supremacy of the Greek spirit. The Etruscans, like the Greeks, were doubtless descended from the old Pelasgians, and recognized in the products brought them by the ships — vases especially, which they bought in large quantities — the encouragement of an effort related to their own. In fact, the most original manifestations of their art always owe something to Greece and, certainly by intermediation of the latter, sleep within them.

Western pediment, temple of Aphaia,
Aigina, c. 500-480 B.C., marble, h: 168 cm.
Glyptothek, Munich

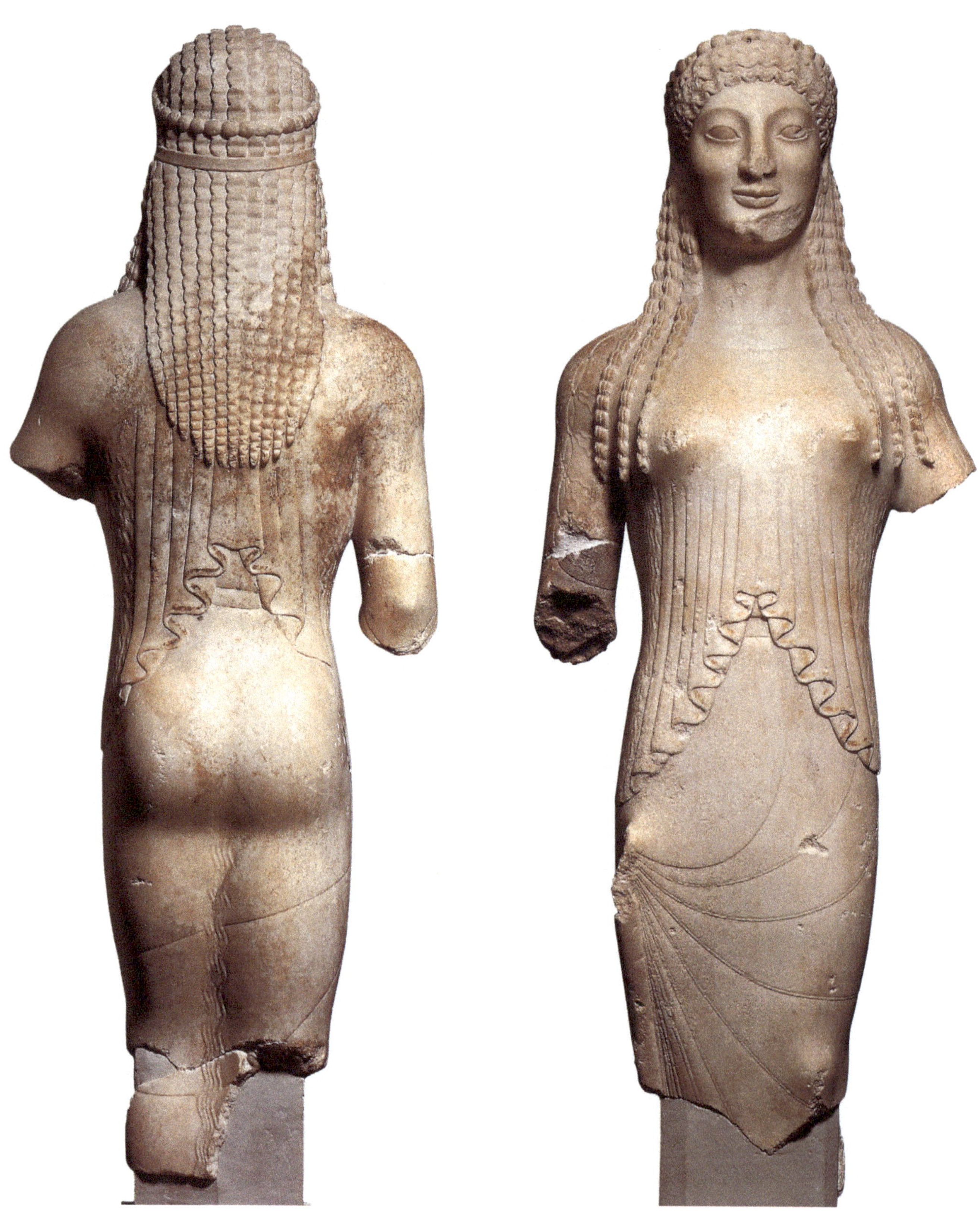

PHIDIAS (C. 480 – 430 BC)

The philosophic sculpture is born of liberty and dies because of it. The slave in Assyria could describe vividly the things he was permitted to see; in Egypt, he could give a definition of form as firm as the discipline which bowed him down, as full of nuances, as moving as the faith which sustained him. The free man alone gives life to the law. The artist of today is afraid of words when he does not fall a victim to them. He is right to refrain from listening to the professional philosopher and specially to refrain from following him. He is wrong to be afraid of passing for a philosopher. Also, if we have no right to forget that Phidias followed the discourses of Anaxagoras (philosopher c. 510 – c. 428 BC), we recognize that he might, without loss, have been ignorant of metaphysics. He looked upon life with simplicity, but what he could see of it developed in him so lucid a comprehension of the relationships which, for the artist, make up its unity and continuity, that minds skillful in generalizing could extract from his work the elements out of which the modern world has come. Phidias formed Socrates (470/469 – 399 BC) and Plato (428/427 or

424/423) – unknown to themselves, doubtless – when he materialized for them, in the clearest, the most veracious, and the most human of languages, the mysterious affinities which give life to ideas.

We see the philosophic spirit as it is born at the beginning of the fifth century, still hesitating and astonished at the daylight; it appears already in the "Charioteer" and in the statues of Aegina. Sculptural science, which is not obliged to copy form, but rather to establish the planes which reveal the profound law of structure and the conditions of equilibrium of form – sculptural science already exists. The "Charioteer" is as straight as a tree trunk; one feels the framework within it, one sees how it is defined by all its contours. It is a theorem of bronze. But in the folds of its rigid robe, in its narrow bare feet planted flat on the ground, its nervous arm and open fingers, in its muscular shoulders, its broad neck, its fixed eyes, and round cranium, a slow wave circulates which – by somewhat abrupt fits and starts – tries to convey from one plane to another the integrally conceived forces of life which determined these planes. The same implacable surfaces, the same harsh passages, are in the warriors of Aegina, with something more; there is here, in the abstract, a course which leads from one figure to another across empty space, and which thus creates a continuing whole, even if still a troubled one, lacking in suppleness and partaking of the mechanical.

◀ **Kore 678,**
Acropolis c. 530 B.C., Athens,
marble, h: 96,4 cm.
Acropolis Museum, Athens.

There is no break in the conditions we are studying. The plastic evolution and the moral evolution mount in a single pure wave. Antenor (mythological figure, counselor to King Priam of Troy) has already erected the Tyrannicides (Harmodius and Aristogeiton both died 514 B. C. became known as the Tyrannicides after having killed the Peisistratid tyrant Hipparchus) on the Agora — the symbolic myths unroll in the frieze of the temples, and the great national wars mingle the divinities with the soldiers, on the pediments of Aegina. The athlete is to become the man, the man is to become the god, until the moment when the artists, having created the god, find in him the elements of a new humanity. Polykleitos (5th century BCE) and Myron (c. 480 BC - 440 BC) have already taken from the form of the wrestler, the runner, the charioteer, and the discus thrower the idea of those harmonious proportions which shall best define the masculine body in its function of uniting strength, skill, agility, nervous grace, and moral calm. To Polycleitus, the Dorian, belong rude and gathered power, virile harmony in repose; to Myron, the Athenian, belong virile harmony in movement, the vigor in the planes of the muscles, which show in a vibrant silence when the contracted tendons press hard on the head of the bones, when the furrows at the bottom of which repose the nerves and arteries, conveyors of energy, hollow themselves out at the moment when the tendons grow taut. The one establishes the profound architecture of the human body, its strength — like that of a bare column — and its visible symmetry, which the gesture and the modeling scarcely break in order that the theorem may be established upon sensation. The other discovers the theorem in the heart of sensation itself, to which the living arabesque returns as a geometrical abstraction,

with the whirl of all its volumes, with the quiver of all its surfaces. By the one, man is described in his stable form, by his vertical frame, by the sheaves of the arm and leg muscles whose precise undulations mark out or mask the skeleton, by his straight belly, broad, sonorous chest, the circle of the collar bones and the shoulder blades carrying the column of the neck, the round head with its glance which continues it without a break. By the other, he is described in his action. It remains for Phidias only to penetrate the statics of Polycleitus with the dynamics of Myron in rounder, fuller masses, defined by planes broader and more mingled with the light — and he has made the marble glow with a higher life and given a heroic meaning to that form and this action. In a few years, which fly with the swiftness of human imagination, anthropomorphism ripens.

On this simple soil, by this healthy race, religious naturalism was to reach its goal of deifying the natural and moral laws as men and women. The poet came, and his symbols gave resplendent visages to these deifications. What the Greek really adored when he was matured and liberated was the accord between his mind and the law. Whatever may have been said of it, anthropomorphism is the only religion that science has left intact, for science is the law deduced from the aspects of life by man, and only by him. Our conception of the world is the only proof we can offer of its existence and of our own.

The personified laws, the gods who have become real beings for the crowd, are not tyrants, not even the creators of men — they are other men, more accomplished in their virtue, more grandiose in their disorder. They have the faults and the impulses of

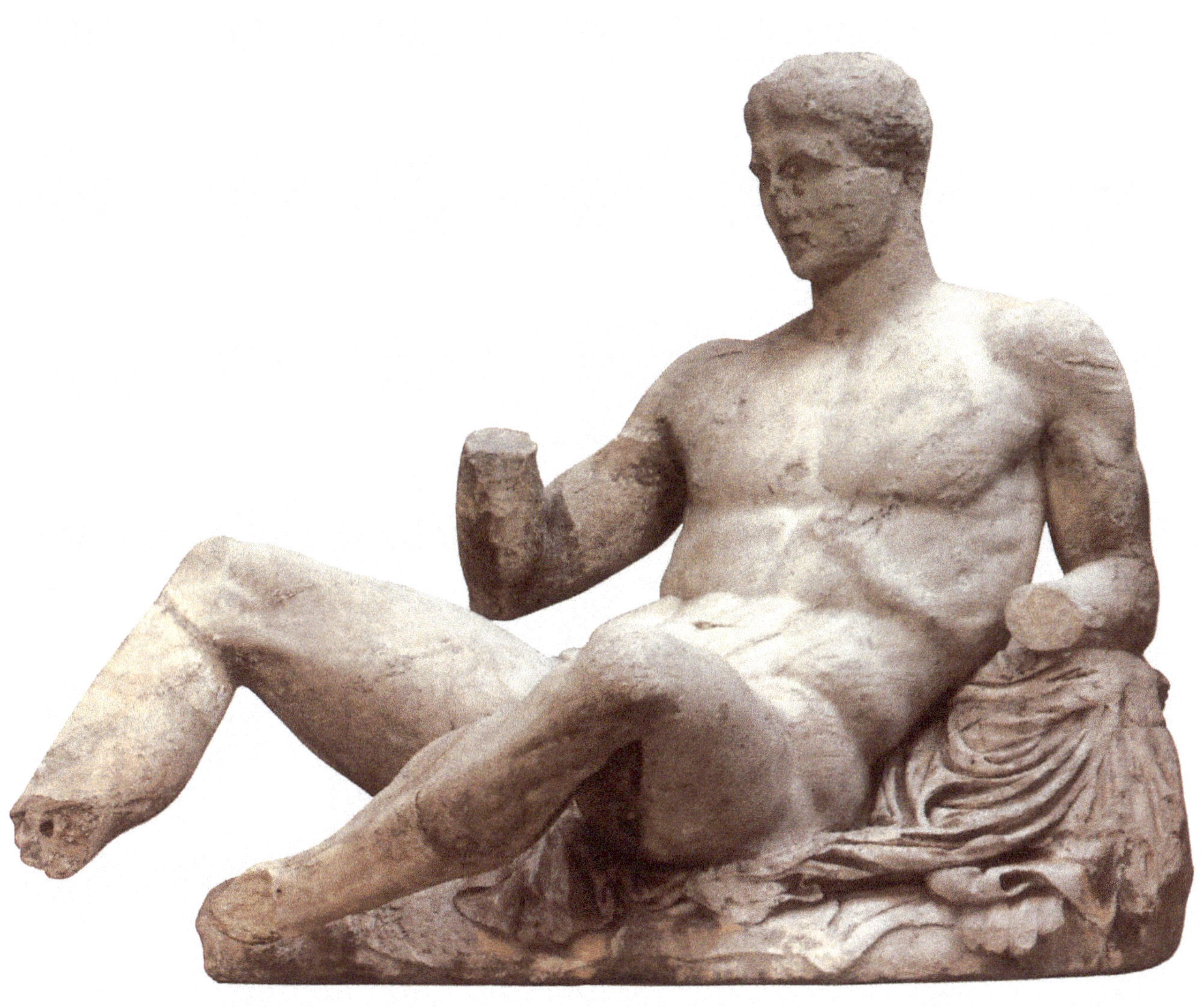

▲ **Dionysos,**
East pediment, Parthenon, Athens, c. 438-432 B.C.
marble, h: 130 cm, l: 200 cm.
British Museum, London.

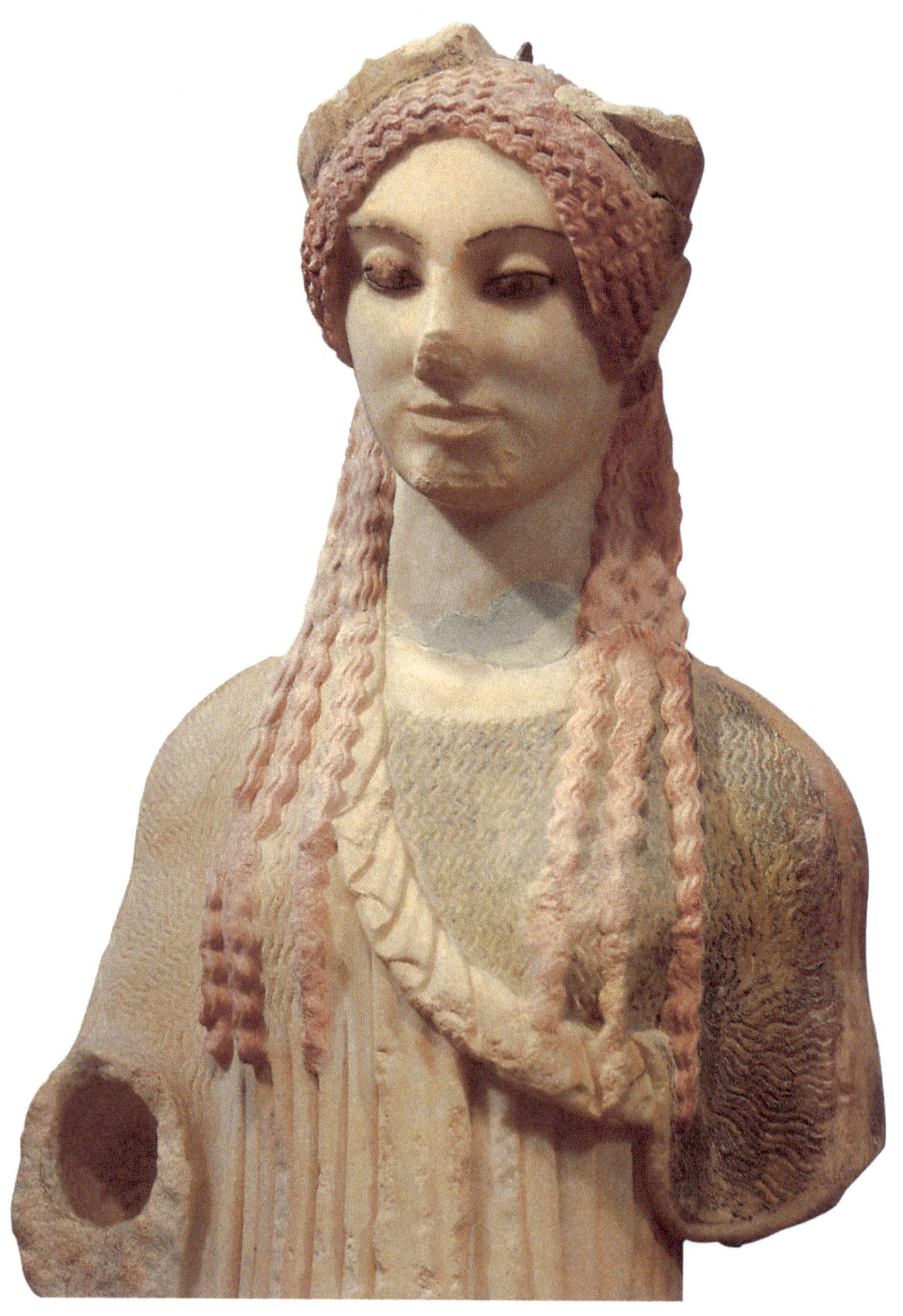

men, they carry the latter's wisdom and beauty to the degree where these become fateful forces, they are the human ideal opposed by human passions. Herakles combats the accident, the thing that retards and opposes our progress toward order. He enters the forests to beat the lions to death, he dries up swamps, he cuts the throats of evil men and overpowers bulls. His hairy arms, his knees, and his breast bleed from his struggle with the rocks. He protects the childhood of the organizing will against the adult brutality of things. At his side, Prometheus (creator of humanity in Greek mythology) starts out for his conquest of the lightning — that is to say, of the mind. The Greek refuses to have anything to do with the god of terrible distances who kills the soul and the flesh through the hand of the priest. He tears the fire from him. The god nails him down with pain, but he cries out in revolt until Herakles comes to cut his bonds. By dint of willing it, man creates his own liberty.

Thus, from the man to the god, from the real to the ideal, from acquired adaptions to desired adaptions, the hero threads his path. The human mind, in a splendid effort, rejoins the divine law. Polytheism organizes the primitive pantheism, and, with admirable audacity and brings out the spirit of it. The sensation of spiritual infiniteness that Egyptian art gives, and of material infiniteness that Hindu art gives, is not to be found in the art that expresses the Hellenic soul. We find in this art an accent of balanced harmony which it alone has, and which keeps within the limits of our intelligence. All forms and all forces are bound together in a deep solidarity; one passes into law, passes into divinity. Doubtless, in the enormous universe of which the city is the definitive image, there are antagonisms, there are action and reaction, but all partial conflicts are effaced and melted in the intellectual order which man founds. Heraclitus has just affirmed, together with the eternal flow of things, the identity of contraries and their profound agreement in universal eurhythm.

It is this, above all, that the old pediments of Olympia came to teach us. Earthquakes have shaken them from their place, man has broken them and dispersed their pieces, the overflow of the Alpheus has washed away their violent polychromy. Even as they are, with terrible gaps, often without heads, without torsos, almost always without limbs, held by iron supports, they remain one, coherent and integral as when, at the foot of Kronion (Mount Kronos) in Altis (sanctuary to the gods), they towered over the forests peopled with statues. Inflamed with passion drunk with wine, the centaurs drag away the virgins. Fists and elbows strike; fingers twist and loosen the grasp of other hands; knives kill, and the great bodies sink under the ax, to the sound of the hammering hoofs, of sobs, and of imprecations. Here everything is rude action, ardor of the new faith, violence of the old myths which retold the tale of the abductions of the primitive forests where all was menace, assault, and mysterious terror. Broad, animated modeling and surfaces cut with great strokes carry out the mood of struggle, of desire, of murder and death.

◀ **Kore 674**,
Acropolis c. 500 B.C., Athens,
marble, h: 96,4 cm.
Acropolis Museum, Athens.

In the sculpture of Olympia there is an enchaining of causes and effects which has its perfect logic, but which is still intoxicated with the discovery of itself. The mind of the artist prolongs it unbroken so that he may gather up into himself its tumult and passion. One moment more and Phidias transforms it into spiritual harmonies which mark the expansion of the intelligence into the fulness of love.

With him modeling is no longer a science, it is not yet a trade, it is a living thought. The volumes, the movements, the surge that starts from one angle of the pediment to end at the other — everything is sculptured from within, everything obeys inner forces in order to reveal their meaning to us. The living wave runs through the limbs, they are instinct with it, rounded or extended by it; it models the heads of the bones and, as ravines cut into a plain, it indents the glorious torsos from the secret belly to the tremble of the hard breasts. The sap, which rises in it and causes it to pulsate, makes of each fragment of the material, even when broken, a moving entity which participates in the existence of the whole, receiving life from it and returning life to it. An organic solidarity binds the parts together triumphantly. A higher life of the soul, for the first and the only time in history merged and confounded with the tempestuous life of the elements, rises above a world intoxicated and strong in the immortal youth of a moment which cannot last.

From the dusk of morning to the dusk of night the pediments spread out their scroll of life. In them, peace descends with the night and light mounts with the day. From the two arms of Phoebus (byname of Apollo), which emerge from the horizon, stretching out toward the peak of the world, to the head of the horse whose body is already in the shadow at the other side of the sky, life grows, marches on without haste, and diminishes. The whole of life. Without interruption these forms continue one another.

Greek art, at this time, reaches the philosophic moment. It is a thing of living change. Idealistic in its desire, it lives because it demands of life the elements of its ideal constructions. It is the species in the law, the man and the woman, the horse and the ox, the flower, the fruit, the being exclusively described by its essential qualities and made to live as it is, in the exercise of its normal functions. It is, at the same time, a man, a horse, an ox, a flower, and a fruit. The great Venus, peaceful as an absolute, is willed by the whole race. She sums up its hopes, she fixes its desire, but her swelling neck, her beautiful ripening breasts, her moving sides make her alive. She lends her glow to space which caresses her, touches her sides with gold, makes her lungs rise and fall. It penetrates her, she mingles with it. She is the unseizable instant when eternity meets universal life.

This state of equilibrium, wherein all the vital powers seem to hang suspended in the consciousness of man before bursting forth and multiplying under definite forms, imparts its force to all Greek art of the highest class. The anonymous sculptor of Olympia and Phidias and his pupils, the architects of the Acropolis, express the same relations, the same prodigious and blended universe brought to the human scale, the same type of reason, superior to the accidents of nature and subordinated to its laws.

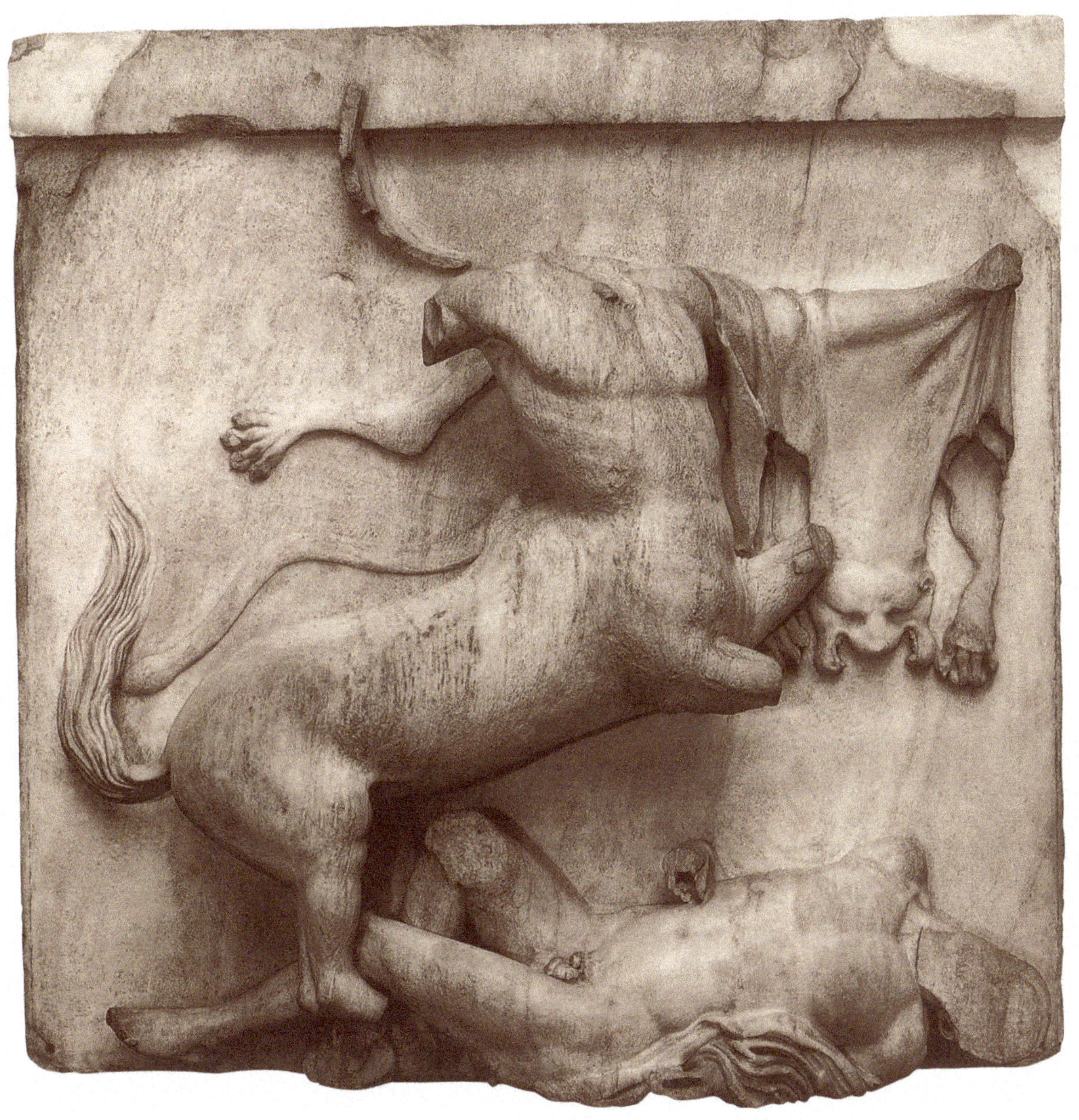

▲ Metope n° 38 on the south side of the Parthenon,
Athens. A centaur stands triumphant over a defeated
Lapith. 446-438 B.C.
marble, h: 135 cm. British Museum, London

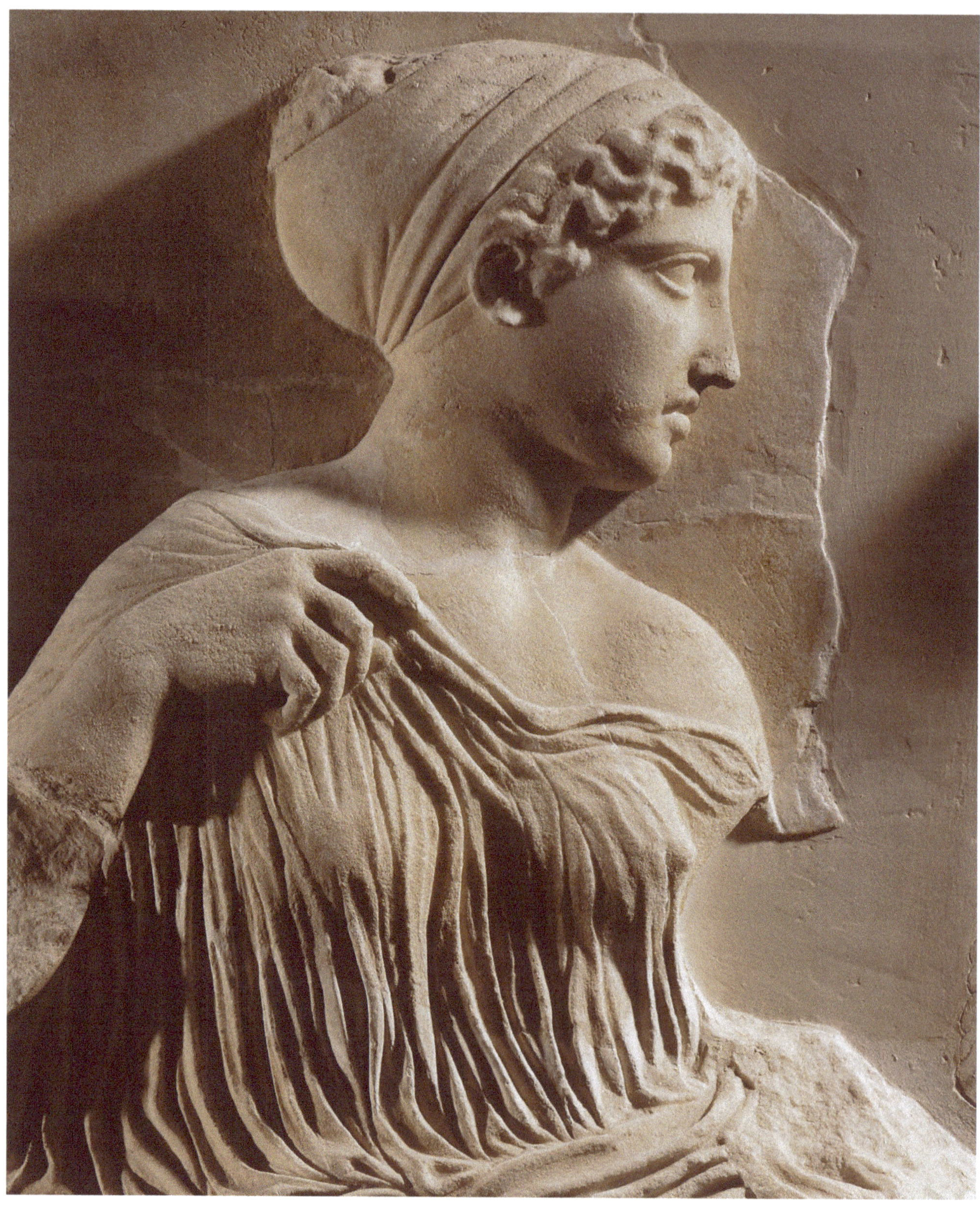

But the language of each one remains as personal as his body, his hands, the form of his forehead, the color of his eyes, the whole of his elemental substance, which is written into the marble by the same stroke that renders the universal order which he has understood and marked with its external form. See the faith, the almost savage sweep of the man who made the statues of Olympia, his rugged and broad phrase. See the religion, the sustained energy, the reserve of Phidias, his long, balanced phrase. See, in the encircling frieze, the discretion of his pupils who have neither his freedom nor his power, but who are calm as he is, because, like him, they live in an hour of certitude.

The bad Roman copies of works belonging to the last period of Greece, the soft goddesses, the draped gods brandishing their lyres, the figures from literature and works of the school have for a long time calumniated Greek art. It expressed to us a colorless people, assuming a theatrical attitude to overawe the future. The artificial heroism hid the real heroism, and the ruggedness and freshness of the primitive were effaced by the fictions of the Alexandrine romancers. The anatomy of the "Theseus" (mythical king and founder-hero of Athens) and the "Ilyssus" (river in Athens) masked the formidable life that swells and dilates them and makes its pulsations pass even to the fragments that have disappeared. The "Panatheniac Frieze"

◄ **Artemis**,
east Parthenon frieze, Athens,
c. 438-432 B.C., marble, h: 100 cm
British Museum, London.

(sculpted between c. 443 and 438 BC), revealed to us the manner in which girls walk as they bear burdens, flowers, and sheaves, how horsemen defile, the tranquility of intelligent strength dominating brute strength, how oxen go with the same step to the slaughterhouse and to work. We had forgotten that these were men and women who had lived, who had loved and suffered, and beasts which used to dig the furrows in the thin plain of Attica, and whose fat and flesh used to burn on the altars.

Democracy is not fully victorious and consequently it is already on the road to decline, but Greece makes the effort from which democracy is to be born. With the wooden idols and the multicolored monsters of the old temples came the death of the oligarchy, the power delegated to a caste which, at bottom, symbolized accepted revelation. Tyranny, which, in Greece, is government by one man whose science has been recognized, the system whose apogee coincides, in the fourth century, with the determination of sculptural science — tyranny is shaken when the movement of life invades the archaic form. The first statues to stir are those of Harmodios and Aristogiton (both died in 514 BC), the men who killed the King of Athens. Then the crushing forces which Aeschylus set like blocks upon the human soul are shaken, with Sophocles (tragedian, c. 497– 406/5 BC) to penetrate one another, to act on one another, and to cause their balanced energy to radiate in consciousness and will. Then Phidias transports into marble the poise of life, and man is ripe for liberty. Democracy appears — the transitory political expression of the antagonism and the agreement of forces in the cosmic harmony.

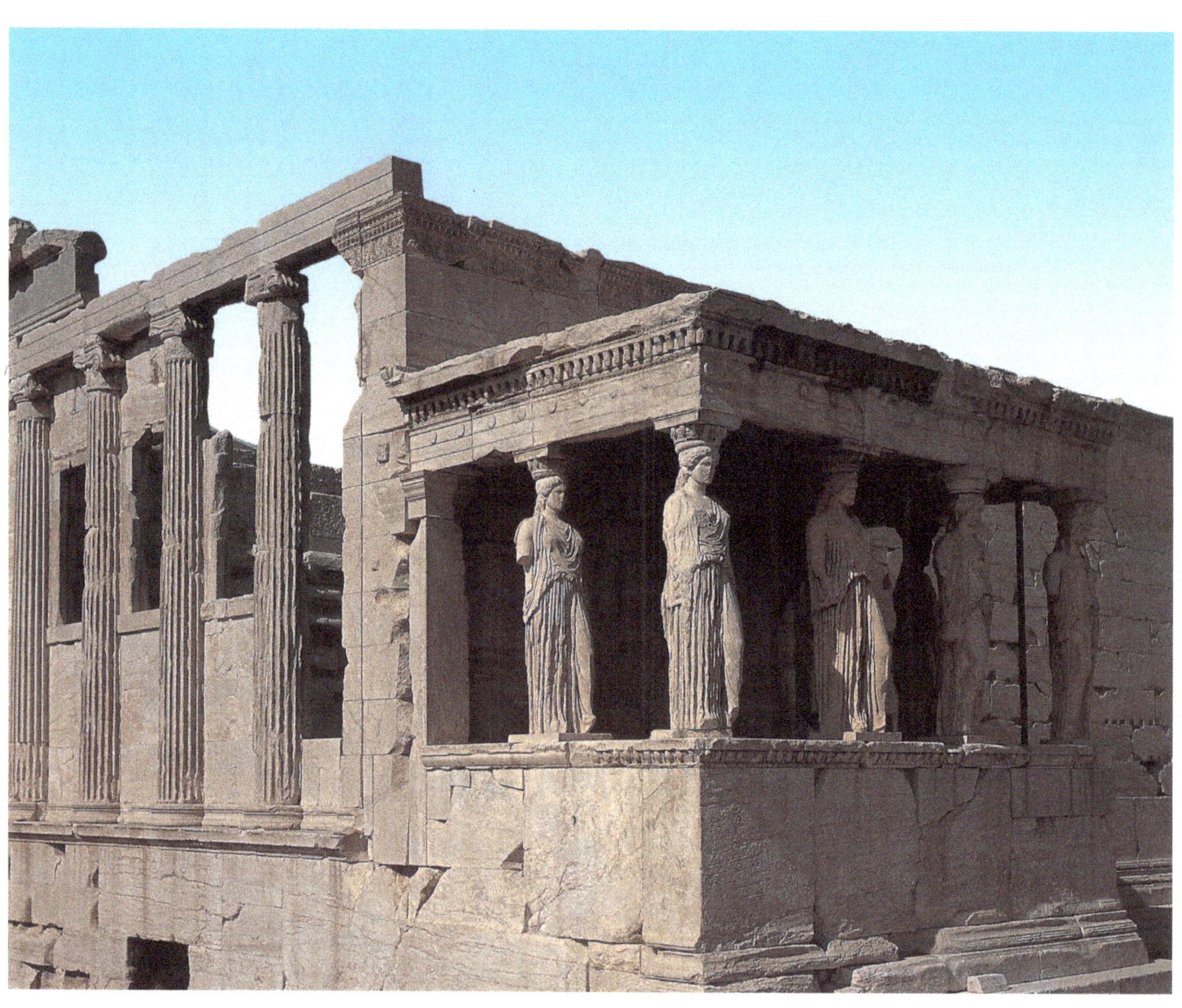

THE PARTHENON

From every Acropolis a Parthenon arises. The chief of the democracy inspires them, the people work at them, the humblest stonecutter gets the same pay as Ictinos (mid-5th century B.C.) the architect, or Phidias the sculptor. At the Panatheniac festivals, with the ritual order ill observed by the enthusiastic populace, in the dust and the sunlight, to the often-discordant sound of oriental music and the thousand bare feet striking the ground, with the brutal splendor of the dyed robes, the jewels, the rouge, and the fruits, the city sends to the Parthenon its hope — with the young girls scattering flowers, waving palms, and singing hymns, its strength with the horsemen, and its wisdom with the old men. The protecting divinity is to be thanked for having permitted the meeting and sanctioned the accord between man and the law.

The temple sums up the Greek soul. It is neither the house of the priest as the Egyptian temple was, nor the house of the people as the cathedral is to be; it is the house of the spirit, the symbolic refuge where the wedding of the senses and the will is to be celebrated. The statues, the paintings— all the plastic effort of the intelligence — is used to decorate it. The detail of its construction is the personal language of the architect. Its principle is always the same, its proportions are always similar, it is the same spirit that calculates and balances its lines. Here the Doric genius dominates, by the austere unornamented column, broad and short; there the Ionic genius smiles in it, through the long column, graceful as a jet of water and gently expanded at its summit. Sometimes young girls, inclining toward one another as they walk, balance the architrave on their heads, like a basket of fruit. Often it has columns on only one or two faces; at other times they surround it entirely.

Whether it is large or small, its size is never thought of. We are tempted to say that the law of Number, which it observes with such ease, is innate with it; one would say that the law springs from this very soil as the shafts rise in their vertical flight between the stylobate and the architrave, that it is the law itself which halts them, and which hangs suspended in the pediment with a sort of motionless balance. The law of Number easily places the temple in

◀ **Erechtheum**,
Acropolis, Athens, c. 420-406 B.C.
In situ.

the scale of the material and spiritual universe of which it is the complete expression. It is on a plane with the day sky, which outlines the regularity of its rectangle in the ring of the horizon of the sea. It is on a plane with the night sky which turns about it according to the musical and monotonous rhythm in which the architect has discovered the secret of its proportions. It is on a plane with the city, for which it realizes, with a strange serenity, the perfect equilibrium vainly sought by its citizens in the essential antagonism of classes and parties.

It is on a plane with the poets and thinkers, who seek the absolute relationship between the heart and the intelligence in tragedy and dialogue, to which it is related by the drama of its sculptural decoration, irrevocably inscribed in its definite order. On the simple Acropolis it is a harmony that crowns another harmony. After twenty-five centuries it remains what it was, because it has retained its proportions, its sustained sweep, its strong seat on the great slabs of stone that dominate the sea surrounded by golden hills. One might say that the years have treated it as they have treated the earth, despoiling it of its statues and of its colors at the same time that they have carried the forests and the soil of the mountains down to the sea and dried up the torrents.

If one has not lived in the intimacy of its ruins, one thinks the Greek temple as rigid as a theorem. But as soon as we really know it — whether almost intact or shattered — our whole humanity trembles in it. The reason is that from its base to its summit the theorem bears the trace of the hand. As in the pediments, the symmetry is only apparent, but equilibrium reigns and makes it live. The laws of sculpture, the laws of nature, are found in it, with logic, the energy and silence of the planes, the quiver of their surfaces. The straight line is there, as solid as reason, the spacious curved line also, reposeful as the dream. The architect secures the stability of the edifice by its rectangular forms, he gives it movement by its hidden curves. The sweep of the columns is oblique; they project a little, one beyond the other, like the trees of an avenue. An insensible curve rounds off the architrave at the line of their summit. All these imperceptible divergences, with the fluting of the columns — a shell which breaks the light, a stream of shadow and of fire — animate the temple, give to it something like the beating of a heart. Its pillars possess the strength and the tremor of trees; the pediments and the friezes oscillate like the branches. The edifice, hidden behind the curtain of the columns, resembles the mysterious forest which opens at the moment one enters it. The temple of Paestum, which is quite black, has the appearance of an animal walking.

Thus, from the living temple to the eternal men who people its pediments and march in the circle of its friezes, Greek art is a melody. Man's action is fused with his thought. Art comes from him, as does his glance, his voice, and his breath, in a kind of conscious enthusiasm; which is the true religion. So lucid a faith exalts him that he has no need to cry it forth. His lyrism is contained, because he knows the reason of its existence. His certitude is that of the regular force which causes torrents of desire and the flowers to spring from beings and from the soil. And the Apollo, who arises from the pediment of Olympia with the calm and the sweep of the sun as it passes the horizon, and whose resplendent gesture dominates the fury of the crowds, is like the spirit of this race which, for a second, felt the reign over the chaos that surrounds us, of the order inherent within us.

A second! no longer, doubtless, and we cannot determine its place. It is mysterious, it escapes our attempt to measure it, as do all human works in which intuition plays the larger part. Did it perhaps burst out in a lost work, perhaps in several works at once. Toward the middle of the fifth century, from the sculptor of Olympia to Phidias, between the rise and the fall, there occurs in the whole soul of Greece an immense oscillation round about this unseizable moment, which passed without her being able to retain it. But she lived it, and one or two men expressed it. And that is the maximum that a living humanity has a right to demand of the dead humanities. It is not by following them that it will resemble them. It may seek and discover in itself the elements of a new equilibrium. But a mode of equilibrium cannot be rediscovered.

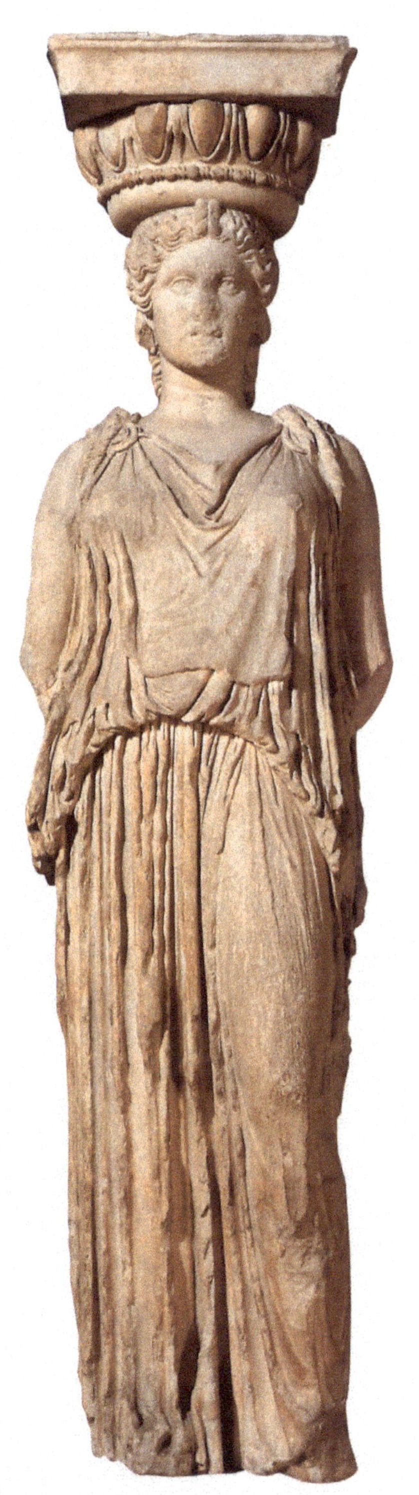

A caryatid, ▶
Erechtheion, Acropolis, Athens,
c. 420-406 B.C., marble, h: 231 cm
British Museum.

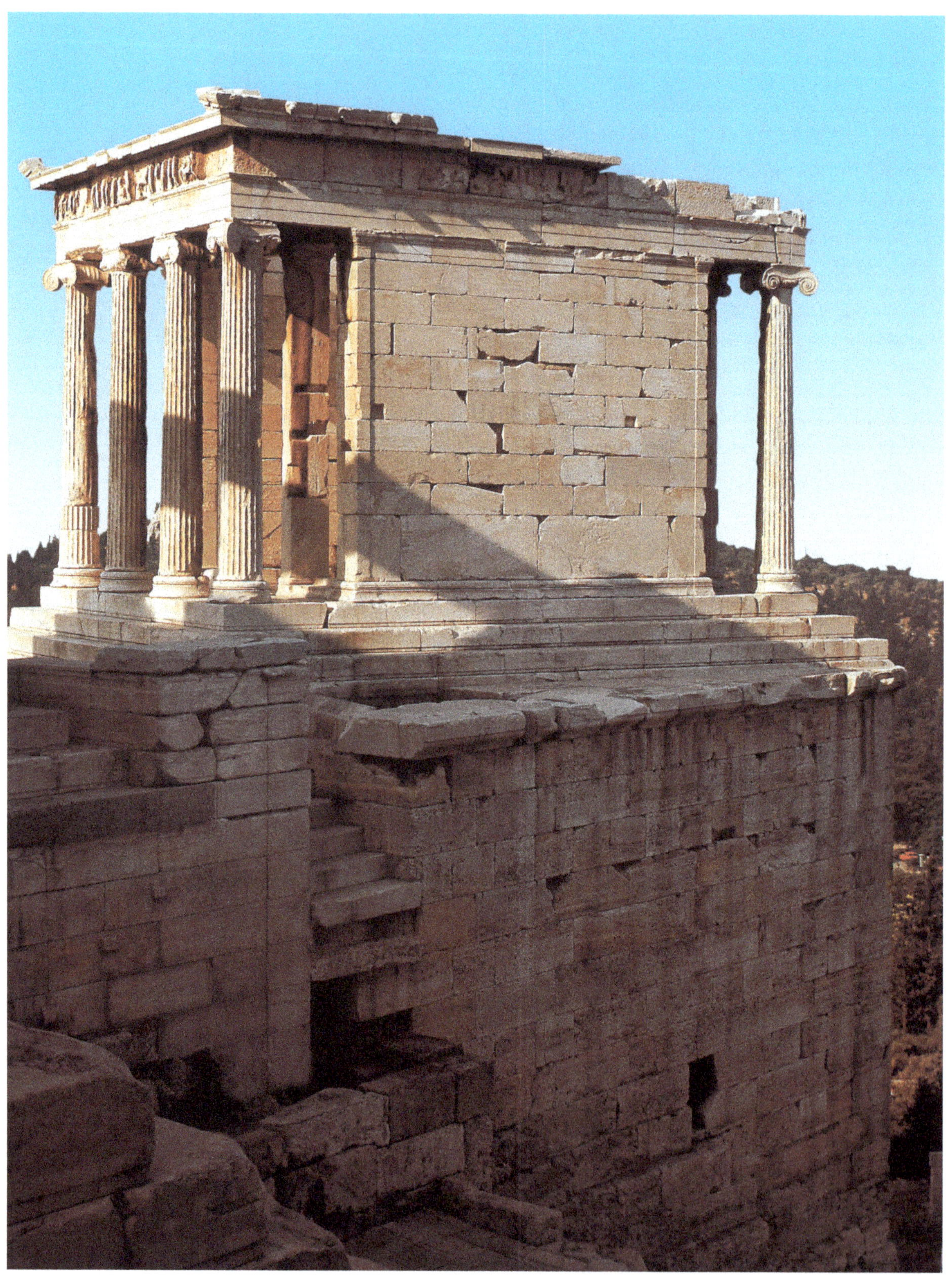

THE DUSK OF MANKIND

The heroic soul of Greece was to ebb away through three wounds: the triumph of Sparta, the enrichment of Athens, and the reign of intellectualism. Sensibility increased at the expense of moral energy, reason overflowed faith, enthusiasm was dulled through contact with the critical spirit. The philosophers, to whose development sculpture had contributed so much by giving life to ideas, were to deny their origin, laugh at the poets and at the artists, and discourage the sculptors through misleading their minds in the meanders of sophistry. We need not bear them a grudge for this. The equilibrium was about to break; no human power, no miracle could have re-established it. And the soul of Athens, on the brink of the abyss to which her logicians were dragging civilization, was even then forging a tool with which the men of a distant future could build a new dwelling. The death struggle of Greece gave us freedom of examination.

Beginning with the last years of the fifth century, a furtive caress passed over the Greek marbles. The great forms, kept alive by the circulation of their inner energies, disappeared from the pediments, and the artist tried to call these energies to the surface of the statues, of the portraits, of the picturesque groups which, however, he isolated little by little. The form and the spirit, which up to that time had flowered in the same integral expression, now separated from each other irrevocably. The spiritualist searched the body to extract the soul, the skeptic no longer tried to derive from it anything more than sensual satisfactions. About that time a little temple was built on the Acropolis to house a wingless *Victory*. But the external victories that had descended upon it had kept their wings. They were to depart from Athens.

Greek sculpture is supposed not to have appreciated the inner life until the fourth century. It might be observed that from the Archaic period onward there are statues, like the Samian woman, or like any Orante (female figure, with outstretched arms) of the Acropolis, whose visage makes us think of that of the Gothic virgins because of their naive enchantment with life which illumines it from within. But that is not the question. People generally believe that thought cannot dwell anywhere save in the head of the model. The truth is that it is entirely in the head of the artist. The inner quality of a work is measured by the quality of the relations which unite its elements and

◀ **Temple of Athena Nike**,
Athens, c. 425-421 B.C.
In situ.

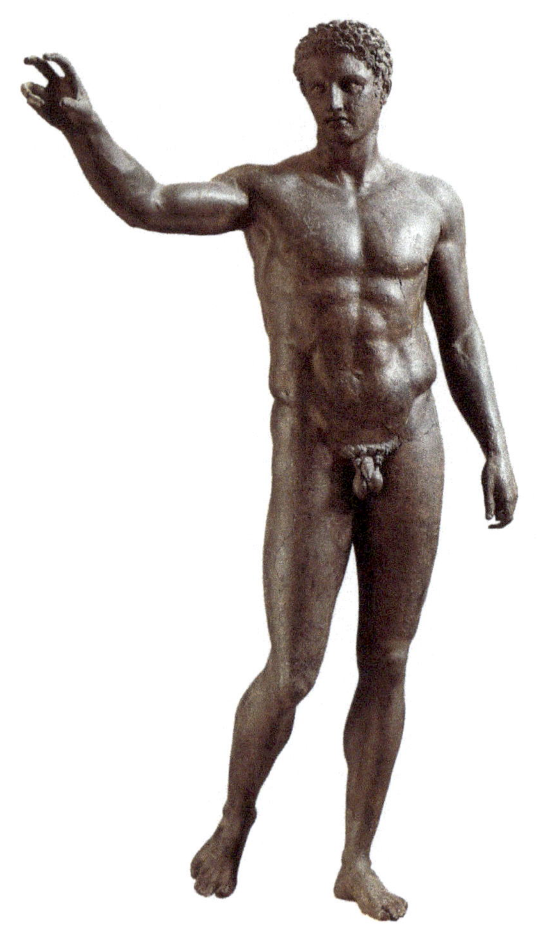

▲ **The Antikythera Youth or Ephebe**,
mid-fourth century B.C.,
Bronze, h: 194 cm.
National Archaeological Museum, Athens.

It is true that in a poor society, where the slave was well treated, where the steps of the social hierarchy were very near together, which lived on an indulgent soil, in a health-giving air, near a flowered sea, human beings did not have an urgent need of one another. The normal expression of man is a resultant of the daily conflict of his passions and his will. The Greek sculptor knew the sentimental agitations whose reflections pass at times over the sternest among human faces. But it was only later, with the definitive breaking of the social rhythm, that these reflections were imprinted there as indelible traces. Man, who was then to be characterized by a warped, suffering body and a haggard face, was defined for Phidias by a complete organic equilibrium wherein the calm of the heart spread through the harmony of the general structure, of which the tranquil face was only one element. The head of the Lapith woman (legendary people of Greek mythology), that of Peitho (goddess of persuasion and seduction), and that of the Artemis (daughter of Zeus) of the Parthenon express a profound life, but a peaceful one. It is like a great depth of pure water, full and limpid and unruffled.

assure the continuity of its ensemble. And no art had more of the inner quality than that of the fifth century. The modeling of everything goes from within outward. The surfaces, the movements, the empty spaces themselves, everything is determined by the play of the profound forces that pass from the artist into the material, as the blood passes from the heart into the limbs and the brain.

Hermes and the Infant Dionysos, ▶
also known as the Hermes of Praxiteles,
Marble, h: 215 cm.
Archeological Museum of Olympia

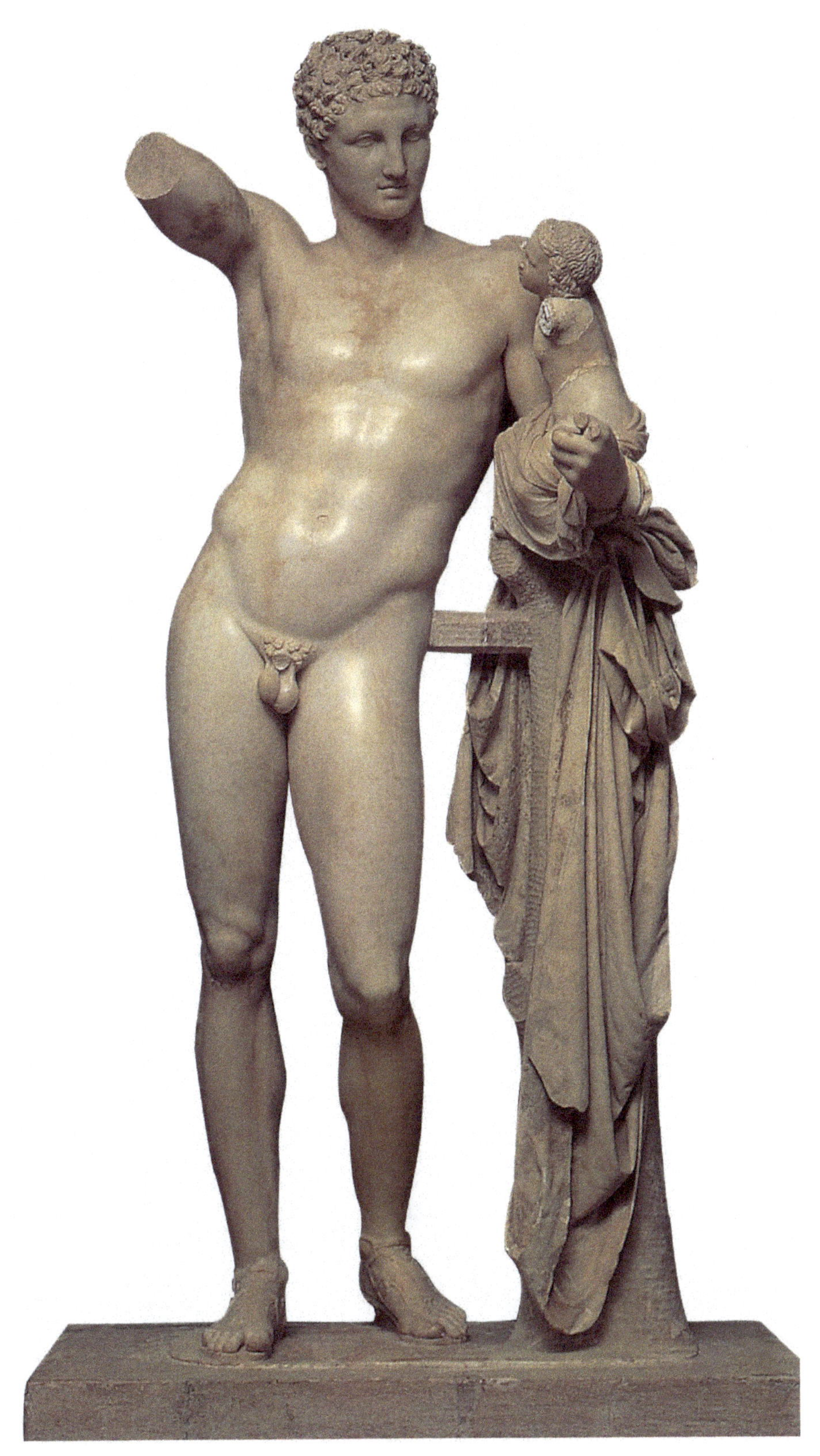

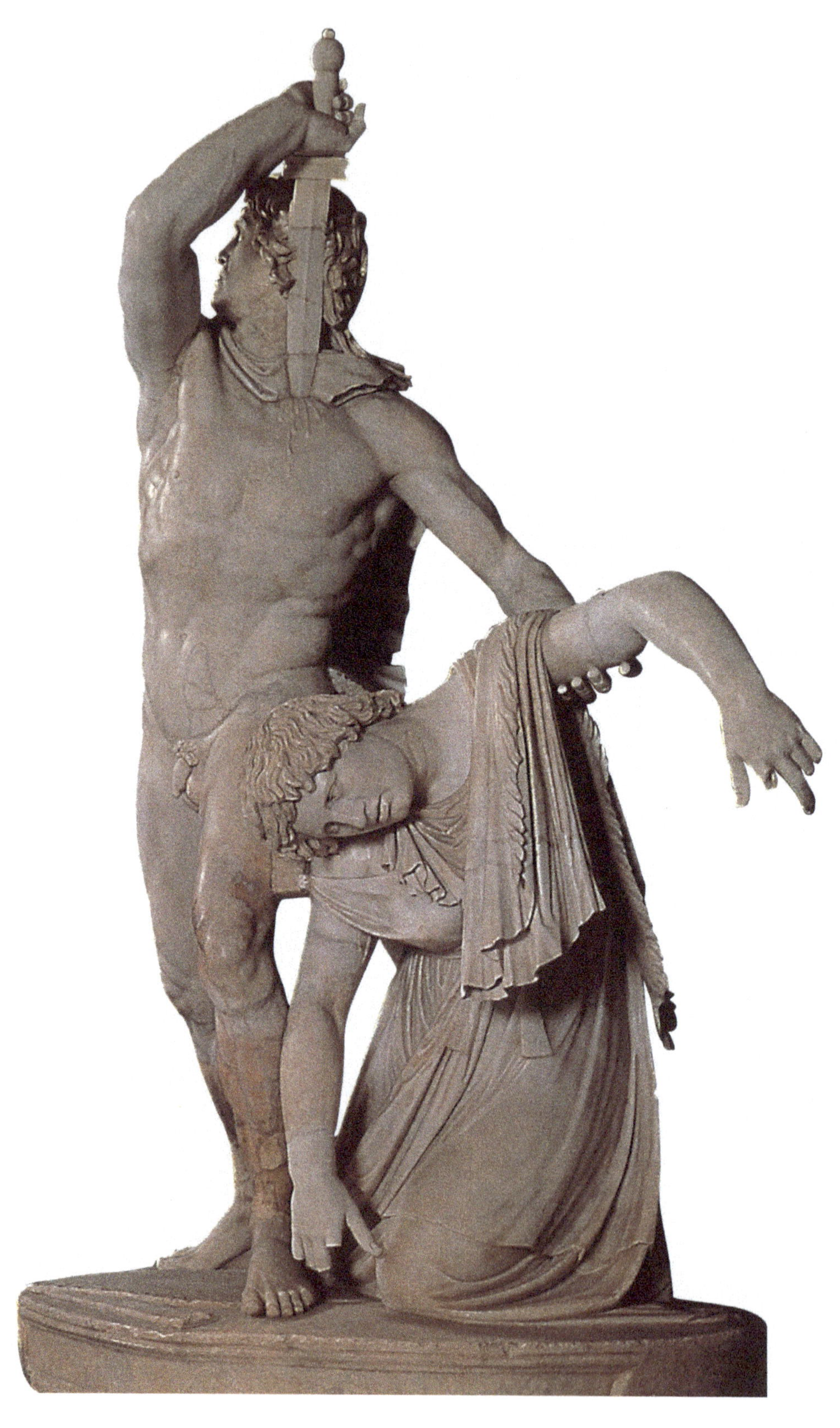

PRAXITELES (C. 400 – BEFORE 326 B. C.)

Praxiteles draws the spirit to the skin of the statues. As he sees the spirit floating on faces as an undefined smile, as a vague disquietude, as a luminous shadow, he fixes it there, and by so doing breaks that unity which gives to the forms of the great century their contained radiance. To express the inner life, he seeks to make it external. And it is no longer as a dawn, it is as an evening that the soul mounts from the depths to spread itself over the surface. Praxiteles is the Euripides (c. 480 – c. 406 BC) of sculpture. His measure, his elegance, his mind, the subtlety of his animation, and the charm of his analysis do not succeed in hiding from us the fact that he doubts his strength, and that, at bottom, he regrets having lost the sacred intoxication at which he laughs. Under his fingers the plane gets soft, hesitates, and gradually loses the spiritual energy with which Phidias invested it. The expression of the form, distraught and as if a little wearied, is no longer the play of the inner forces, but that of the lights and shadows on its shell. The soul seeks to escape from the embrace of the marble. One

◀ The Ludovisi Battle sarcophagus,
replica after a Greek original
Under the king Attalus I and Eumenes II, c. 220 B.C.,
marble, h: 211 cm. Museo Nazionale Romano, Rome.

sees this clearly in the great dreamy foreheads under the wavy hair, in the sensual and vibrant mouth, in the undefined charm of the face as it leans forward. That no longer means intelligence; that means sentiment. Art dies of it, but new life takes its germ from it and, much later and under other skies, is to flower from it. At the moment when human language and enthusiasm weaken together, the work of Praxiteles affirms, not the appearance, but the survival of the mind and a kind of transference of its function, which is to spend many long centuries in searching for its real organ and in the end, is to find it.

His art betrays the coming of a kind of cerebral sensualism which we see appearing at the same hour among all his contemporaries, to whom the friezes of the temple of the "*Wingless Victory*" and the capital of the "Dancers" at Delphi had already shown the way. Little by little, the deep structure is forgotten, so that the surface of the figures may be caressed by desire, as the surface of the faces is marked by the artist's effort to depict psychological states. When the statue remains clothed, the robe becomes lighter than a breeze on the water. But, for the first time, the Greek sculptor wholly unveils woman, whose form is significant more especially through the tremor of its surface, just as the masculine form, which had dictated his science to him, is above all significant through the logic and the rigor of its structure. For the first time he rejects the stuffs which the pupils of Phidias had begun to drape in every direction, at the risk of leaving unexpressed the life moving under them. It is without veils that he expresses the movement of the torsos as they draw themselves up to their full stature, the animation of the planes which the light and air model in powerful vibration, the youth of breasts, the vigor of masculine bellies, and the pure thrust of arms and legs. He speaks of the body of woman as it had never been spoken of before, he raises it up and adores it in its radiant warmth, its firm undulations, in its splendor as a living column through which the sap of the world circulates with its blood. These mutilated statues confer on the sensuality of man the highest nobility. Full and pure, like a well of light, entrusted by all their profiles to space which is motionless about them, as if filled with respect, these great forms sanctify the whole of paganism as, later, a mother bending over the dead body of her son is to humanize Christianity. And if we are intimately grateful to Praxiteles and regard him with a tenderness which does not resemble the heroic exaltation to which Phidias transports us, it is because he has taught us that the feminine body, by its rise into the light and the affecting frailty of the belly, the sides, and the breasts in which our whole future sleeps, sums up human effort in the unconquerable idealism with which it faces so many storms. It is impossible to see certain of these broken statues where only the young torso and the long thighs survive, without being torn by a tenderness that is sacred.

But the early fervor is soon to be transformed; something a little wearied is to touch the force of the marble. Very quickly the forms lengthen, become slenderer, flow like a single caress, and tremble with sensual agitation, with shame invaded by love. The modeling undulates gently, the passage becomes insistent, insinuates itself, and, little by little, effaces the plane. Wandering hollows dapple the skin, the breasts are uncertain flowers which never quite open, the neck swells as if with sighs, the knot of hair secured by the fillets weighs on the beautiful round head over which the tresses course like a stream. As at the end of Egypt, it is the troubled farewell to woman, a farewell in which sleeps the hope of distant resurrections. Look, after seeing the "Victories," after the "Dancers" of Delphi — so natural in their grace that they make one think of a tuft of reeds — look at the "Leda" as she stands to receive the great swan with the beating wings, letting the beak seize her neck, the foot tighten on her thigh — the trembling woman subjected to the fatal force which reveals to her the whole of life, even while penetrating her with voluptuousness and pain.

Thus, through criticism and sensuality, Greece came to study the actual man and to forget the possible man. Lysippus began again to cast athletes in bronze, muscular and calm young men, whose immediate life, no longer the inner one, goes no deeper than their rippling skin. The form, indeed, is always full and pure; it is dense and unsettled, but

The Cnidian Aphrodite, ▶
Roman marble copy of an original by the ancient Greek sculptor Praxiteles (torso and thighs) with restored head, arms, legs and drapery support c. 350 B.C., Museo Pio Clementino, Vatican

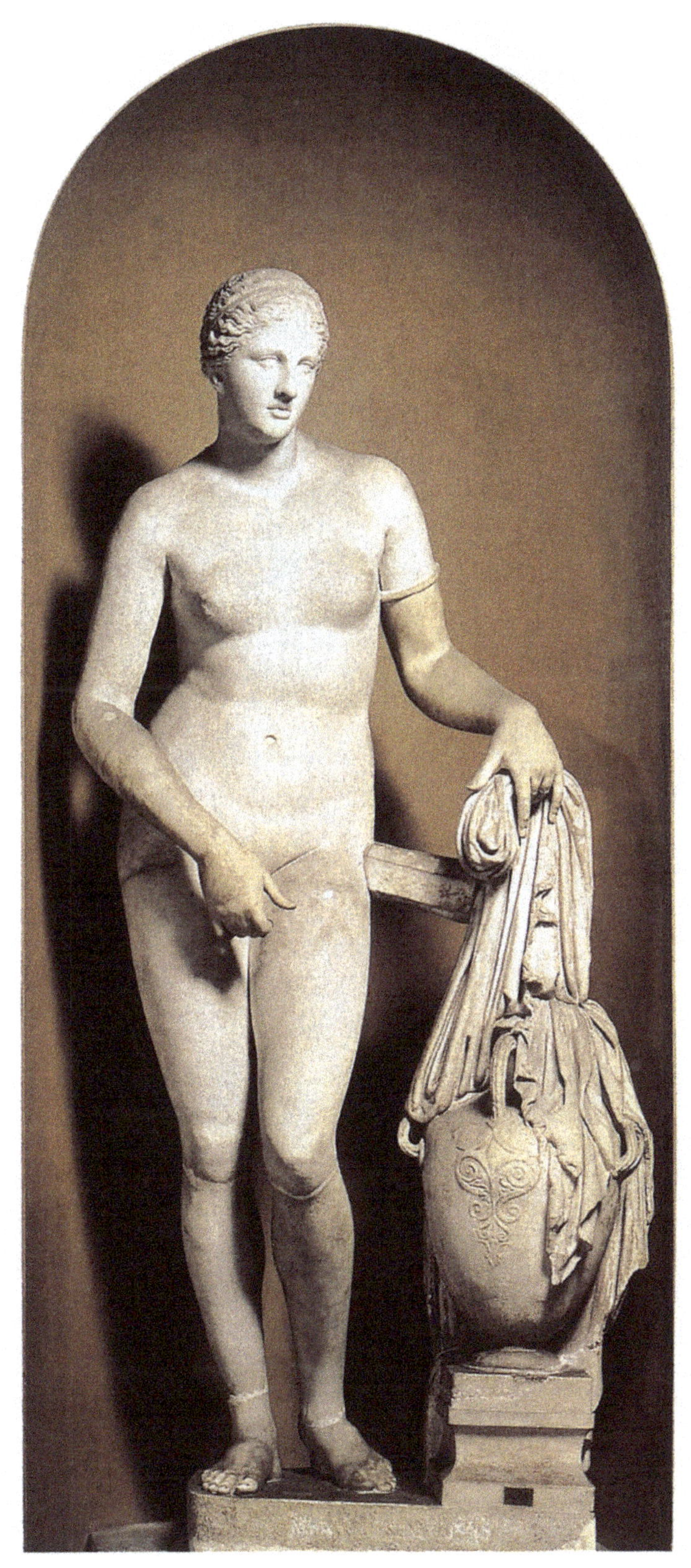

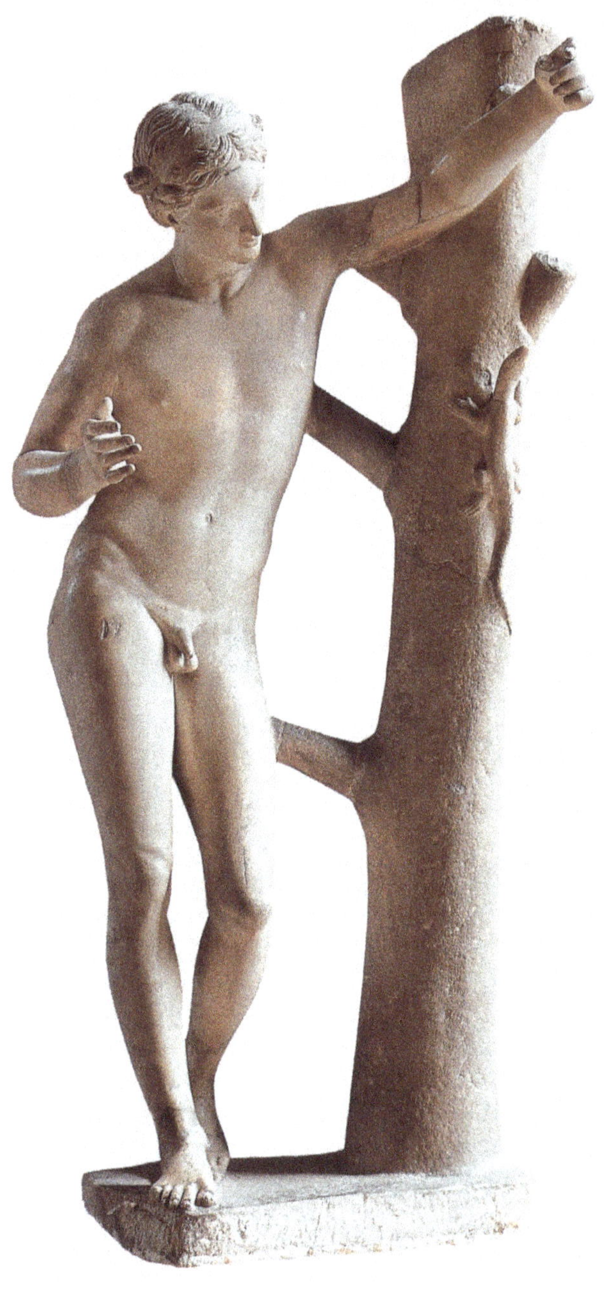

coherent, and has the look of a thing conceived as a whole. When these athletes left the stadium, they seemed to descend from the temple, so well did the serenity, the assurance of their strength, still concentrate in them. But the hieratic idea of the first periods of sculpture, the divine idea of the great century, no longer interposed between them and the statue maker, who saw them directly. At the same time and by the same means he turned his sculpture toward those character portraits which, in reality, we know only by the Roman copies. The earlier ones — that of Homer (author of the Iliad and the Odyssey), for example — reveal to us disenchanted nobility, discriminating fineness and reserve. But later we find fever, excessive sensitiveness, and virtuosity in description. It is a movement, moreover, which announces the gravest social crisis. Art is no longer a function of the race; it begins to make itself dependent on the rich man, who is to turn it away from its heroic course more and more, to demand of it portraits and statues for apartments and gardens.

The last of the great monuments of the classic epoch, the Mausoleum of Scopas (famous architect and sculptor, c. 395 BC – 350 BC) and Bryaxis (sculptor, first half of the 4th century), is made for a private individual. King Mausolus (377–353 BC), and, by an irony which partakes of the symbolic, this monument is a tomb. It is living, certainly — nervous, sparkling, and impregnated with intelligence. In the warriors, in the Amazons and their horses, in the races, the flights, and the attacks, there circulates a free, proud and delicate spirit, a rapidity of thought which almost forestalls the action, which brings into the material the resonance of the armor, the neighing of the horses, the sound of their hoofs beating on the ground, and of the vibrations of javelins and tightly drawn bowstrings. The chisel attacks the marble with the conquering fire of a too ardent mind in anxious haste to set down at the flood tide of its excitation, an enthusiasm already tainted with doubt. With its extreme elegance of form, its sharp mordant expression, and its direct gesture, it is a cool breeze that crosses an early evening. There is constant parallelism between fold and fold, between limb and limb, between movement and movement. The empty spaces are very empty, we no longer feel the passage of that abstract wave through which the volumes penetrated one another and, from end to end of the pediment, gave the effect of a sea whose crests brought with them the hollows — which heave to a crest again. The hollow is isolated here, the wave is isolated; picturesque and descriptive detail profits by this dissociation to appear and impose itself. It is to tend, more and more, to predominate over the philosophic ensemble.

The evolution of the great periods is approximately the same everywhere; but in Greece from the seventh to the third century it appears with an astonishing relief. Man, when he realizes himself, proceeds like nature, from anarchy to unity, from unity to anarchy. At first the scattered elements have to seek one another in the darkness of the mind. Then the whole mass of the chaotic creature is weighed down by the soil, which clogs its joints and clings to its heavy steps. Then the forms disengage themselves and find their proper places and agreement; their logical relationships appear,

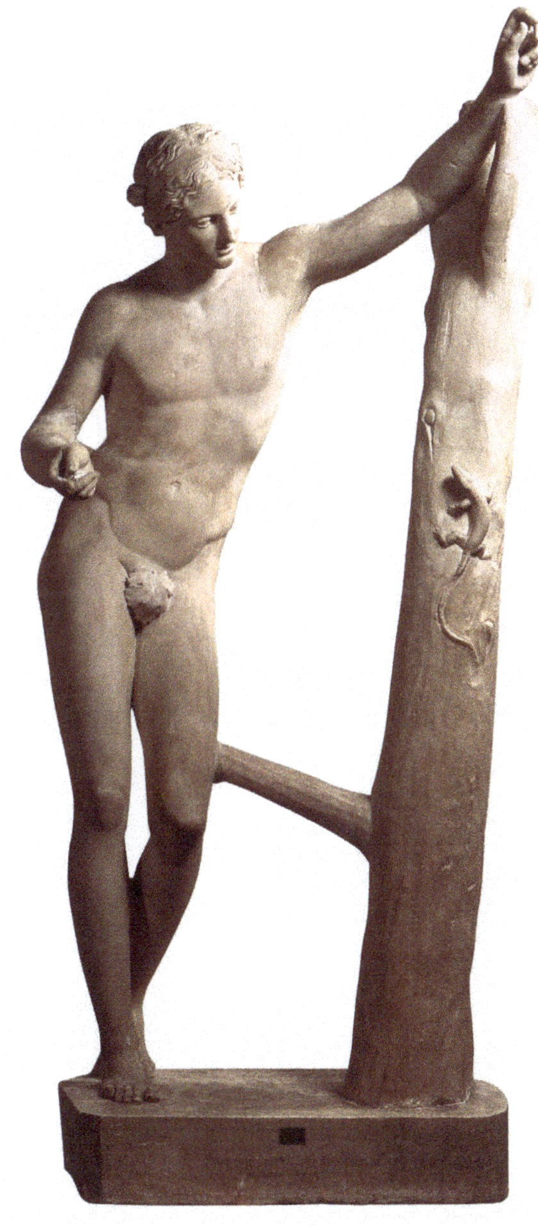

▲ **The Apollo Sauroktonos**,
Roman marble, copy of an original by
the ancient Greek sculptor Praxiteles, marble,
fourth century B.C., Museo Pio Clementino, Vatican.

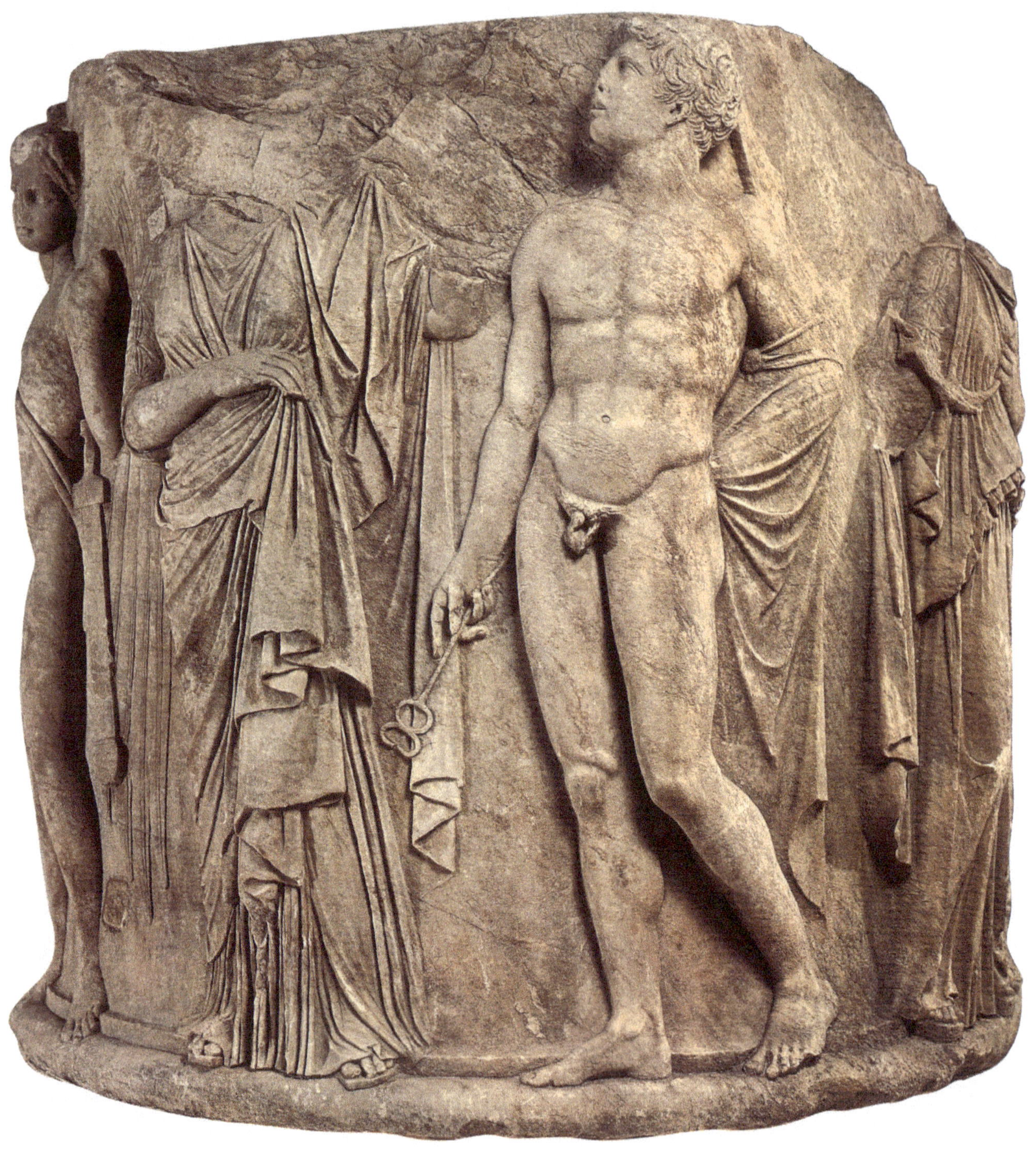

and each organ adapts itself more and more closely to its function. In the end the rhythm is broken, form seems to flee from form, the mind seems to wander at random, the contacts are lost, the unity disintegrates. Thus, there are in Greek art four definite epochs: The Primitives, Aegina, the Parthenon, the Mausoleum. First, the stammering analysis followed, with the Archaic men, by a brief and rough synthesis. Then, when the mind is mature, a new and short analysis, luminous and compelling, which ends, with a single bound, in the conscious synthesis of a society in equilibrium. Finally, a last research which Is not to reach its goal, which is to dissipate itself more and more until it has reduced its fragments ad infinitum, has broken all the old bonds, and has, little by little, lost itself through lack of comprehension, fatigue, and the urgent need of a great, new power of feeling. His forgetting of the essential relations causes the artist to become concerned over the accident, the rare movement, the exceptional expression, the momentary action and, most of all — when men turn back to the horizon of the mystical, the artist's solicitude takes the form of looking for fright, pain, delirium, for physical suffering, and sentimental impulses of all kinds. The plastic synthesis undergoes the same disintegration. It is then that detail appears; it tyrannizes over the artist. The attribute invades the form. The latter gesticulates in vain as if it wanted to defend

◀ **Thanatos,**
Alcestis, Hermes et Persephone, column base,
Temple of Artemis, Ephesus, c. 350-300 B.C.
Marble, h: 155 cm. British Museum, London.

itself, the attribute rivets itself on like a chain. Lyres, tridents, scepters, lightnings, draperies, sandals, headdresses — the whole rag bag of the studios and the theatrical dressing-room makes its entrance. The deep lyrism of the soul subsides, there is need for an external lyrism to mask its exhaustion. It was enthusiasm that made the statue divine; how is the god to be recognized now if he has no scepter and no crown? Faith uplifted the material and made light zoning flash from it to the very heavens of human hope. That is over with. The statues need wings. In the fifth century the wing was rare on the shoulders of the gods. It was to be found among the Archaics as they tried to tear form from the chains of matter. It is found among the decadents where it tries to raise the form, whose own ardor no longer sustains it. The "Victory of Samothrace" already has need of wings to rise from the prow of the ship, because of the complication of the wet draperies which weigh on her legs and make heavy her terrible sweep, the turn of her bust, and the tempest of flight, of clarions, and of the wind that rises in her wake.

Greek art, at the very moment that it was thus breaking up in depth, was scattering over the whole material surface of Hellenic antiquity. After the movement of concentration that had brought to Athens all the forces of Hellenism, a movement of dispersal began, which was to carry from Athens to southern Italy, to Sicily, to Cyrenaica, Egypt, the Islands, and Asia Minor the passion and, unfortunately, the mania, for beautiful things — in default of creative genius. Dilettantism and the diffusion of taste multiply and at the same time weaken talent. It is the Hellenistic period, perhaps the richest in artists and in works of art that history has to show, but perhaps, also, one of the poorest in power of emotion.

There are few men to listen to the voice within them now, and, in a brief rush of fervor, occasionally to catch from it — like the vigorous sculptor of the *Venus of Milo* — a very noble, if somewhat dulled and disunited, echo of the hymn to life whose triumphal choir dies out in the past. The adroit and active author of the "*Sarcophagus of Alexander*" takes the subjects of the old Assyrian sculpture, for lack of its science, and transforms its force and its brutality into somewhat declamatory lyrical movement. The sculptors of Rhodes, especially, seek gesticulating and complicated melodrama in the sensational event and in literature, so that they may be surer to touch popular sentiment, which is beginning its reaction against the skepticism of the philosophers. Others, who cannot see significance in the normal manifestations of life, lure the patron by making their work tell anecdotes for him. We reach the irritating reign of the picturesque little groups. They are still charming sculpture, to be sure, of a learned and witty elegance, but without the naive quality, and already announce monotonous factory work, trinkets, art for the amateur, and those coffins of the artist's dignity, the glass case, the shelf, and the collection.

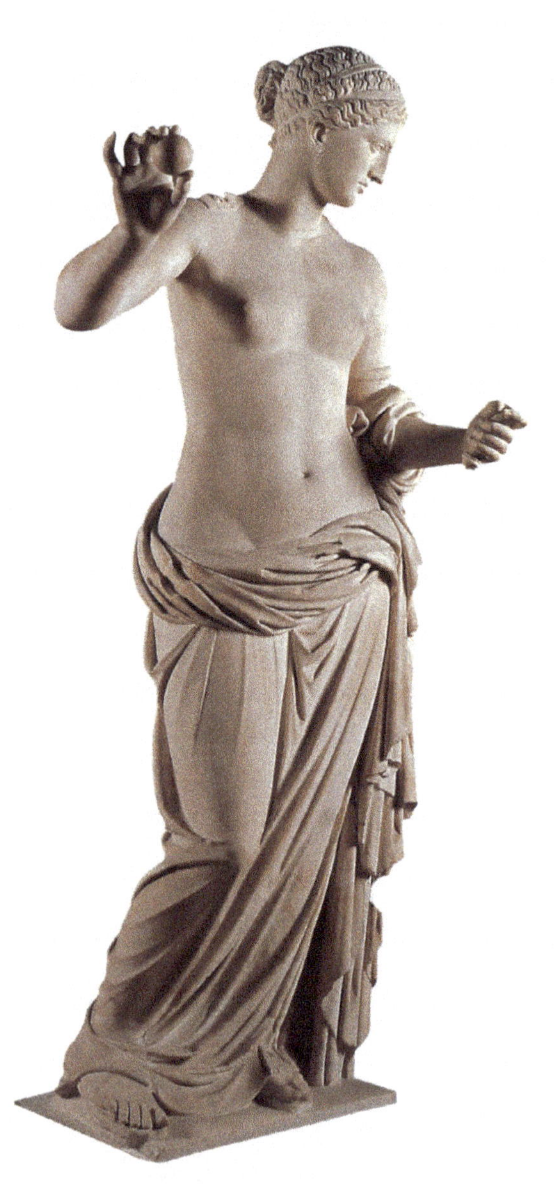

▲ **Aphrodite,**
called the Venus of Arles, copy of the Aphrodite of Thespiae by Praxiteles, end of the 1st century B.C., Marble, h: 194 cm. Musée du Louvre, Paris.

The Apollo Belvedere, ▶
c.120–140; copy of bronze original of c. 350–325 B.C.
Marble, h: 224 cm.
Museo Pio Clementino, Rome

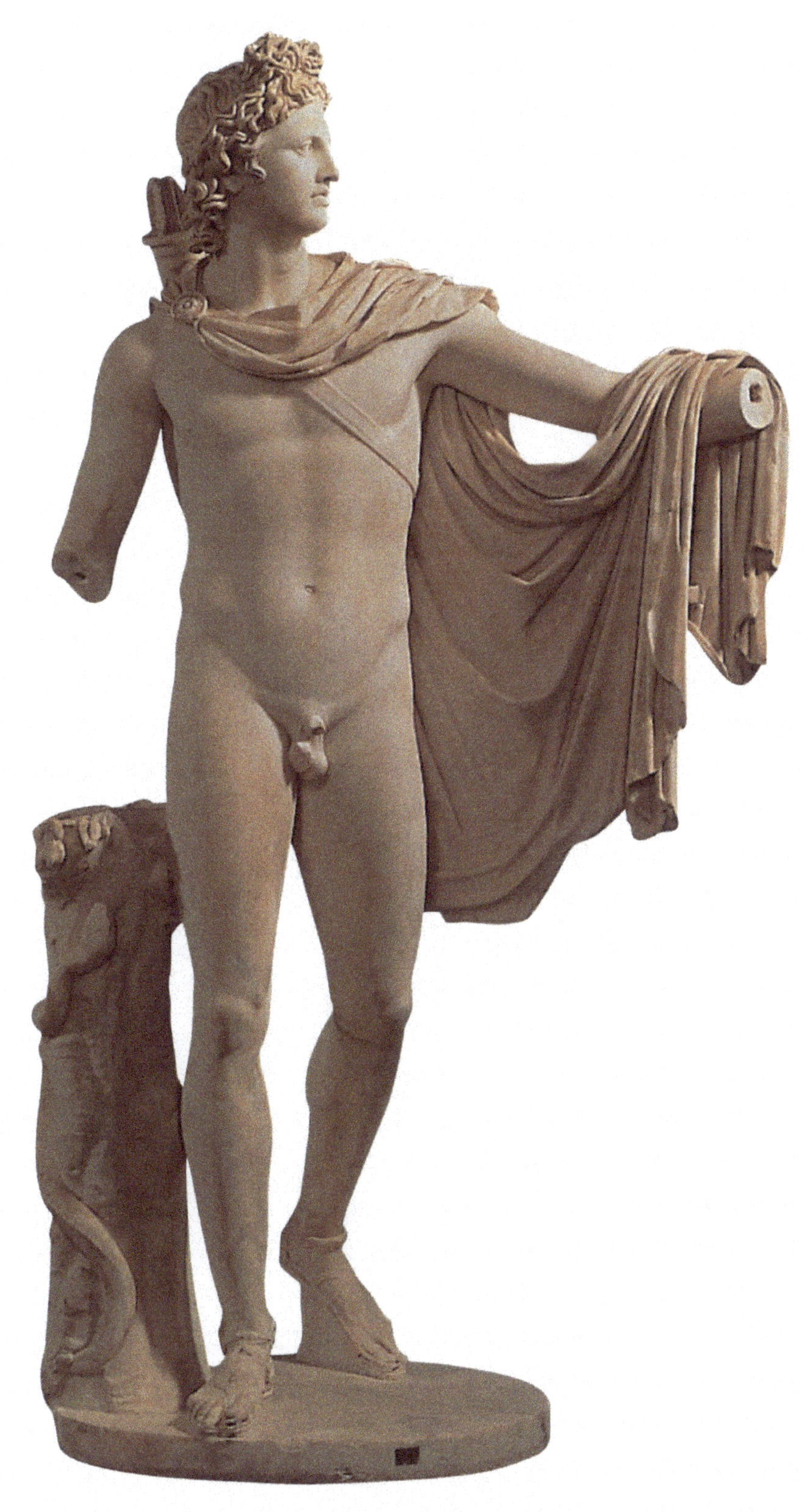

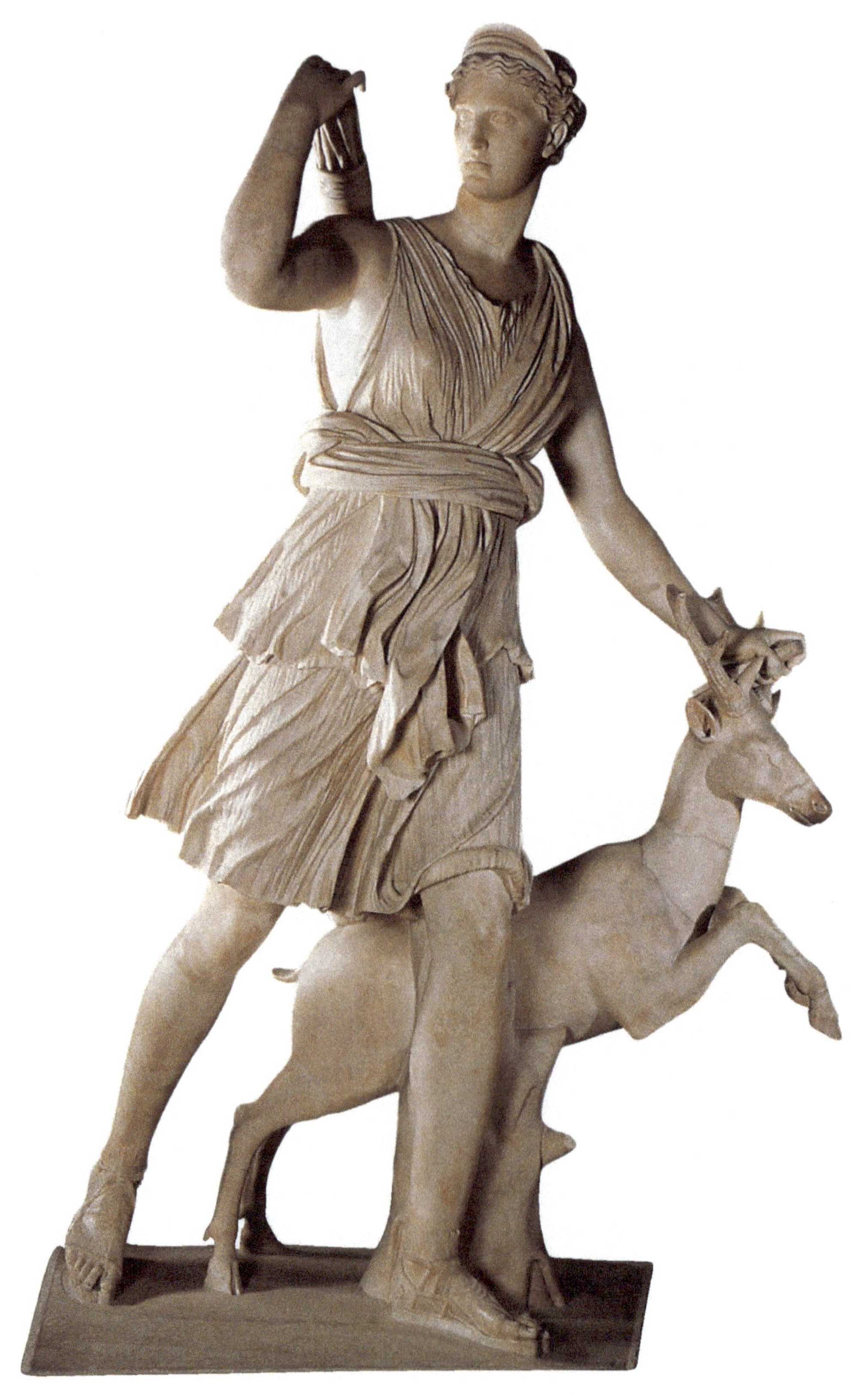

THE GODS HAVE DESERTED THE SOULS OF THE ARTISTS

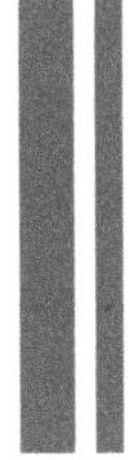

These undefined currents, dominated by the sentimentalism of the middle classes and the elegant lassitude of the blasé, act one on another, in harmony or in opposition, and follow or push back in every direction the hesitating wave that goes from the shores of Asia to the shores of Egypt, from Pergamos to Alexandria, from the islands to the three continents. The incessant mixing of the populations of the coasts produces a wild maelstrom in which some waves from the depths, bringing back the violence and heaviness of Asia, arouse the passion of humanity to the point of desperation. But the Greek soul is no longer anything but a foam evaporating on the surface. Man has lost his unity. His efforts to seize it again only plunge him into deeper night. The Altar of Pergamos, the last of the great collective designs that Hellenism has bequeathed to us, is the image of this disorder. Where sobriety had been, there is heavy luxuriance; confusion replaces order; the rhythm grows wild and breathless; melodramatic effort stifles all humanity, and oratorical power becomes emphasis and bombast. The artist, in the abundance of his speech, exhibits the noisy emptiness of his mind. His speech is ardent, without doubt, sumptuous in color, trembling with his clamor and his gesture, but it is a little like a mantle loaded with gold and gems that has been caught by the wind. Scopas (c. 395 BC – 350 BC) had, at least, no fear of open spaces in his groups; he was too much alive; the sap of the primitive had not abandoned him; when he had nothing to say, he held his peace. But the sculptor of Pergamos is afraid of those great silences through which the spirit of Phidias, when it left one form to go toward another, glided on its invisible wave. The sense of spiritual continuity is so foreign to him that he does not hesitate to replace it by the factitious continuity of external rhetoric. He fills the backgrounds, stuffs the holes, and chokes up every bit of space that he can find. When a man has little to say, he talks without a stop. Silence bores only those who do not think.

Man is to wander despairingly for ten or twelve centuries in the night that falls between them. Already the authors of the melodramatic groups of the "*Laocoon*," the "*Farnese Bull*" and the romantic suicides are no longer sculptors, but bombastic play-actors. Feeling, which is to be reborn in the crowds, is dead in the image cutters, who have been domesticated by the powerful. Even their science

◄ **Artemis**,
the Diana of Versailles, marble, Roman copy of the Greek bronze original attributed to Leochares,
c. 325 B.C., h : 200 cm. Musée du Louvre, Paris.

is dead. The statue maker is hardly more than a diligent anatomist, who follows exactly the relief of the muscles and the dramatized movement that fashion prescribes for his model. Sculpture does not even think of recovering something of the lost paradise through divine irony, for which it is not made. But through irony Lucian of Samosate (c.125 AD – after 180 AD) is to console minds from which pitiless rationalism has driven out faith. The gods have deserted the souls of the artists to dwell in the hearts of stoics, who welcomed them without a word.

There is to be, indeed, during this slow, irremediable wasting away of the Greek idea, some moments where the decline is arrested, some startled gestures revealing a momentary return of vitality; occasionally a few green shoots come from the old transplanted tree. Nothing dies without a struggle. Upon coming into contact with newer races, the Hellenic genius, ashamed of its decay, attempts a vigorous return to itself here and there, and if it does not bring the gods back to earth, it sees, living on the earth, a few heroic forms around the flourishing cities and the illumined bays. To follow its infiltrations through the Latins of northern Italy and the Latinized colonies of the valley of the Rhone is rather difficult, the more so because, from the origins of Greek civilization, Magna Graecia had not ceased to cultivate thought, to cut marble, and to cast bronze. Paestum in its swamps, and the temples of Sicily on their soil of lava and Sulphur, where the herds of goats wander amid the cactus, bear witness to the fact that a collective power reigned. It was triumphant over wars, it defined the idealism of the race even more than it did the character of the cities. The evolution of the Hellenic desire had been everywhere the same. Magna Graecia had bared its goddesses to discover the woman in them at the same moment that Praxiteles had. But perhaps it had grown soft more quickly, as if submerged in voluptuous and enervating, luxury. Southern Italy was richer than Greece, more fertile, less rugged, and more generously supplied with orange trees, with flowers, and with breezes. The beautiful statues of Capua have the fluidity of perfumed oils and the polish of the skin of courtesans; they are without any strength of their own, their modeling melts and flows like wax. Rome had little trouble in subjecting those who lived among them.

This need of fusing the two great modes of plastic evocation had been appearing in Greece itself for at least three centuries. Praxiteles looked on form as a painter rather than as a sculptor; Lysippus (4th century BC), also, at times, and the sculptor of the *"Tomb of Alexander,"* and especially the decorator of Pergamos. The great classic sculpture had indeed made use of painting, but as an accessory means, to give to the form, already living through its own structure, the superficial appearance of life. Under the broad, simple tones which covered the decorative ensembles and remained tranquil in the light, the sculptural plane persisted. On the contrary, in the fourth century, and very much

Aphrodite of Milos, ▶
known as the Venus de Milo, c. 100 B.C.,
Marble, h: 202 cm.
Musée du Louvre, Paris.

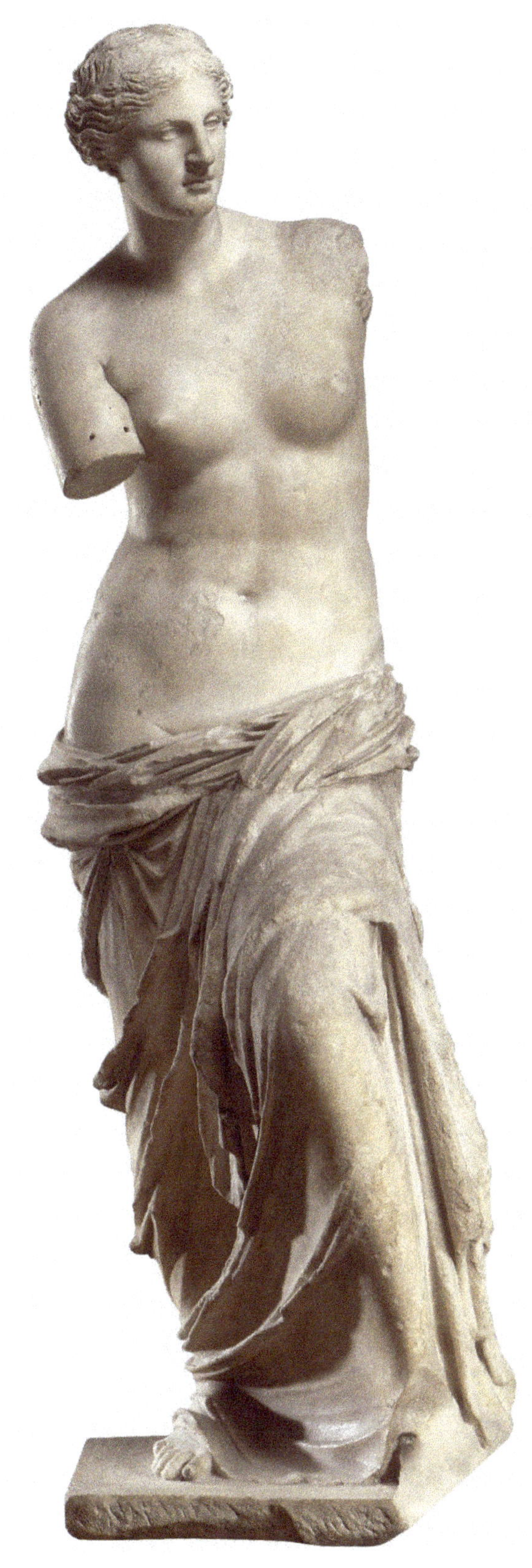

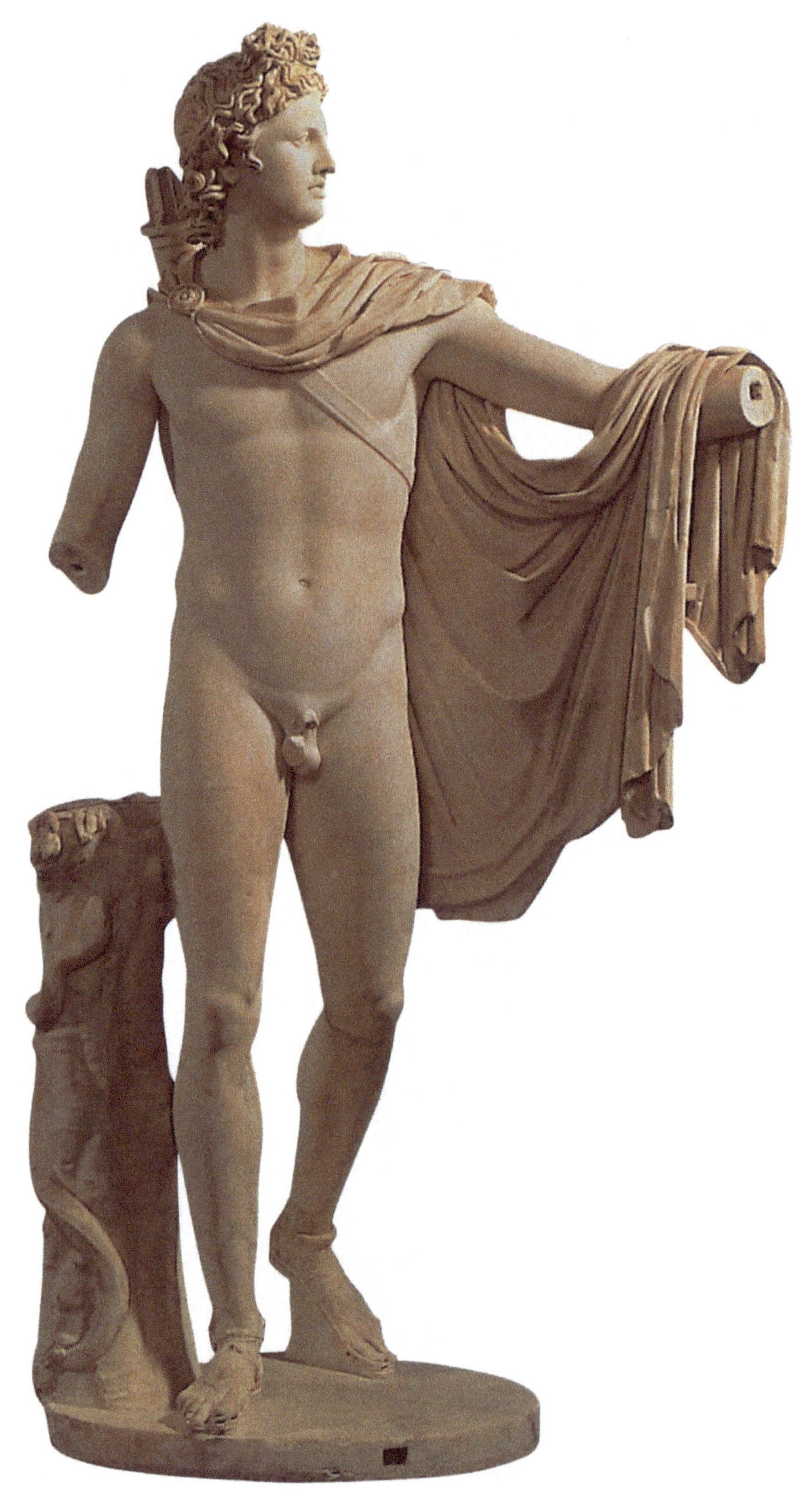

more in the Hellenistic periods, pictorial expression tends to get along without form and to model the surfaces by the mysterious play of the lights, the shadows, the half-tones, and the diffused envelope of the air. It is still a legitimate process when it is practiced on bas-relief, but it is fatal to sculpture. Form must live in space by its own means, like the living being. The planes determined by its inner life are the exact criterion of the statue's success or failure in its contact with the outside atmosphere. An envelope is necessary only to the painter, since he transfers conventionally, to a flat surface, the materiality and the depth of space. If the sculptor incorporates an artificial atmosphere with form, the real atmosphere will devour it.

The ideal of the Greek is wisdom, the order of the world obeyed and disciplined by the intelligence, the conquest — patient and undivorced from life — of a relative equilibrium. He has a strong feeling for what is just, but what is beautiful and what is true is to the same degree the object of his passion. He finds in each of these ideas the echoes of the other two, and completes, tempers, and broadens each one through the others. Phidias is in Pythagoras (c. 570–495 BC), and Socrates is in Phidias,

The Jews were bound to misunderstand Christ because he reacted as an artist against the ideal of justice which had made them unjust, and

c. 120–140; copy of bronze original of c. 350–325 B.C.,
Marble, h: 224 cm.
Museo Pio Clementino, Rome

taught the lowly to pity the strong. The Greeks were far better prepared to understand Him. They knew Him from long ago. He was Dionysus (god of the grape harvest), come from India and returning through Asia with the armies of Alexander (356 BC – 323 BC); Dionysus the god of periodic resurrections, the god of primitive superstitions, of magics and sorceries, as he had been, in the time of Aeschylus, the god of pagan drunkenness; Dionysus, the eternal god of the multitudes and of women. He was the God-man of their myths also, the hero, Herakles, Prometheus. Before Christ the Stoics had taught the conquest of the inner freedom, which is the measure of the discipline which we can impose on ourselves. Before Christ Socrates had died for man. The humanity of Christ was the testament of the ancient world rather than the preface to the new. On the western soil, plowed by Greece, the real thought of Christ is to be reborn in the speech of Prometheus, after more than a thousand years of darkness, furies, and misunderstanding. Perhaps it is this abyss that is contemplated by the old portraits of the last Egypt, with their faces of enigma and their shadowy eyes in which a light trembles.

It has been said that Greek art lacked character. To assert this is to know it inadequately, and perhaps only by the calumnies which the academies, the Roman copies, and the retrospective novels have spread about it. What is character? It is the placing in evidence not of the picturesque, but of the descriptive elements of a given form. The art of the fifth century, which has been said not to have character, goes beyond individual character. It expresses the entire species, it describes it by insisting upon the dominant character of every individual. But the intimate art of Greece does not aim so high. With its charming wisdom, it follows individual character. People have forgotten the Greek portraits — so rare, it is true, but so penetrating— they have forgotten the Tanagras (Greek terracotta figurines), the Myrinas, the vase paintings, the whole of Pompeiian painting, and those statuettes, those studies which perpetuate the cruel satire on the life of the sick, the hunchbacked, the lame, and the infirm of all kinds. They forget that there are even caricatures in the sepulchers of Tanagra. The popularity which the comedies of Aristophanes enjoyed is explained when we know their spectators. There was plenty of laughter in Greece, the philosophers laughed at the gods, the people laughed at the philosophers. The coroplasts (figure makers) of Tanagra and the potters of Ceramica were wholly joyous.

The cult of the stone for its own sake, for its arresting of light, was unknown to ancient art. The material must be wrought, must have imprinted in it man's idea of the universe, of himself, and of his destiny. In stone, in marble, bronze, gold, silver, ivory, wax, wood, and clay, in all the crystallizations of the earth, its bones, its flesh, its blood and its tears, the Greek of every land carved the form of his spirit. Some men have doubted the beauty of the chryselephantine sculpture of the fifth century as they have doubted the splendor which the temples of blue and gold must have taken on as they arose, under the immense Greek sky, from the forests and laurels of the acropolises and the promontories, giving to the white marble an indescribable -quality of absolute spirituality. When they carved

Athena (goddess of wisdom, craft, and war) and Zeus in ivory or gold, the Greeks wanted only to express their veneration for them. But a mind like that of Phidias could not be mistaken in the medium. Behind his brow reigned order, lyric force, and the harmonious accord between intelligence and the heart, and if he carved gods in gold and ivory it was because gold and ivory obeyed him as marble did. What difference does the material make? Whatever it is, it expresses the artist as, in the crust of the earth, coal, and the diamond mingle and expresses its subterranean fire. The material is poured boiling into the mold of his soul; when his soul is strong, clay is strong as bronze, and when his soul is gentle, bronze is as tender as clay.

What good stuff the world is made of! Like the skin and the wool of the beasts, like the meat of the fruits, like bread, this stuff is man's companion. It is the water and the salt. It has the docility of the domestic creatures, it welcomes the master at his threshold and at his doorstep, protects him in the walls and the roofs, offers itself for his repose, hollows itself to receive his food, reaches up to lift its fruits to his lips and strives ingeniously to yield him materials less hard than itself. There was a time, toward the end of Hellenism, when wrought material surrounded man on every hand, like a motionless procession, at once defending and exalting him. Heroic art was weakening, doubtless,

Laocoön and His Sons, ▶
various dates have been suggested for the statue, ranging from about 200 .B.C. to the 70s A.D., marble, h: 184 cm. Museo Pio Clementino, Vatican.

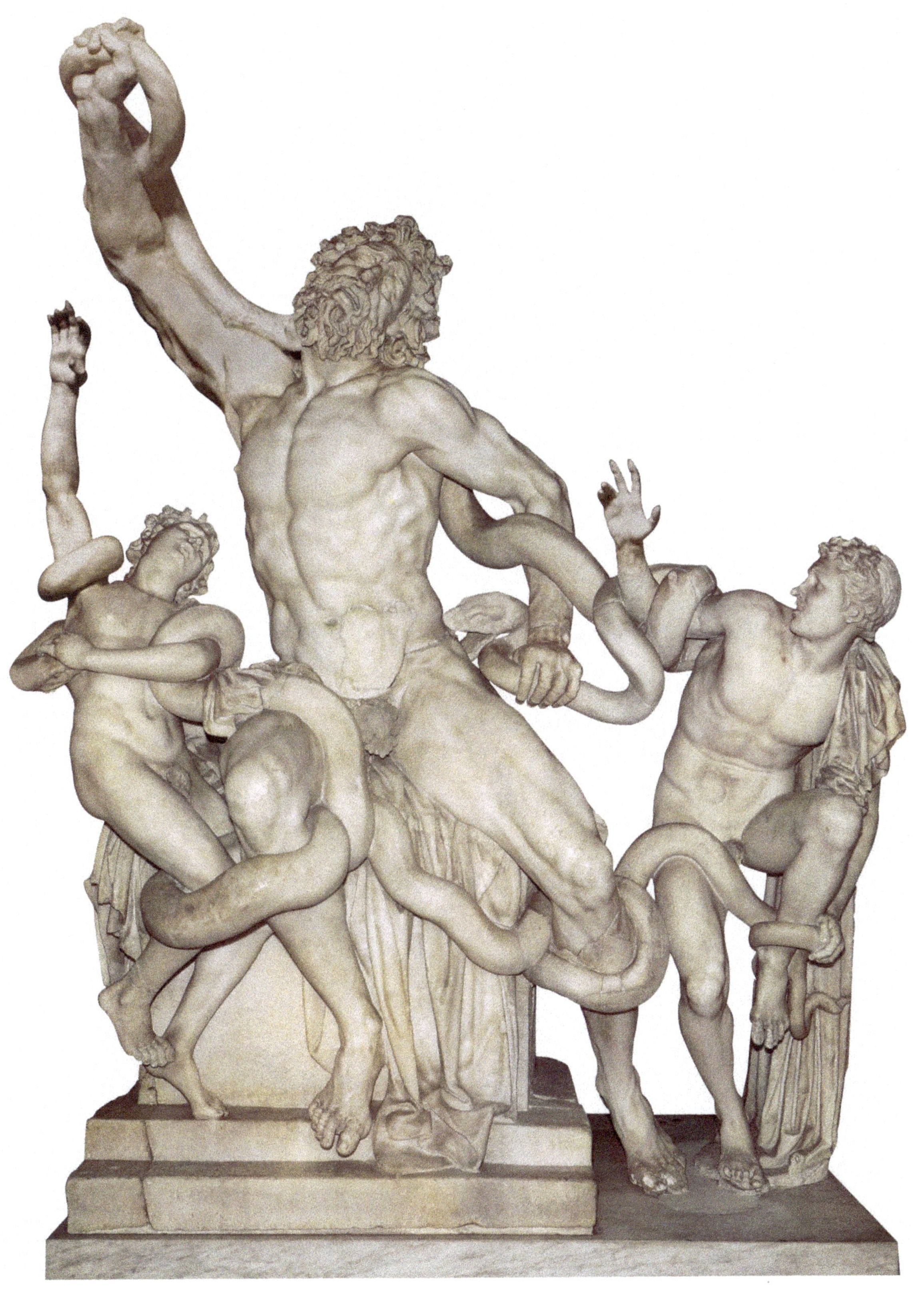

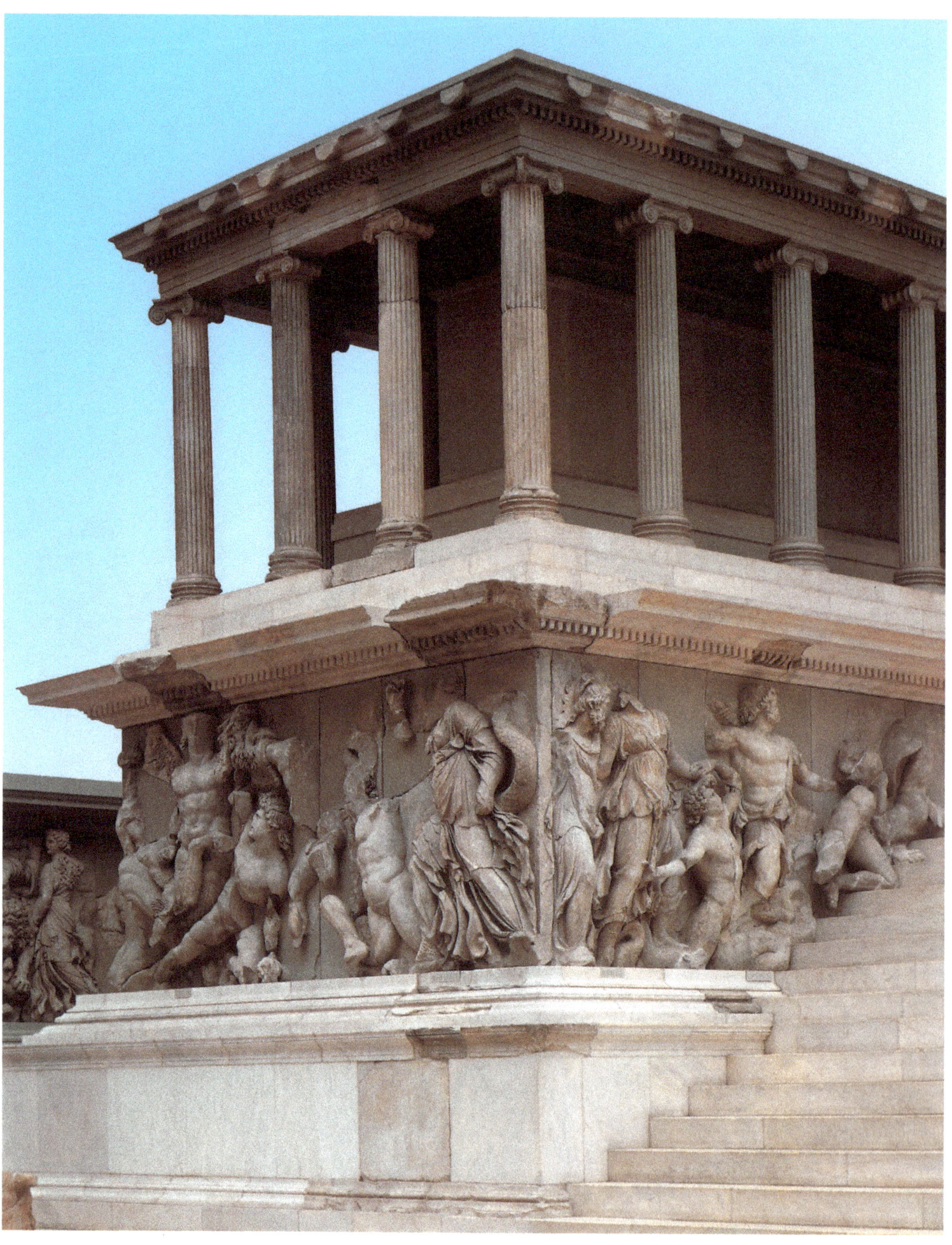

but the gods of ivory and gold were intact, deep in the sanctuaries, and the bright-painted marble heroes still inhabited the metopes where the gold of their bucklers glistened. Painted temples were everywhere, and porticos, stadiums built of steps, colonnades, and terminal gods. The pavements of the streets were of marble, as were the steps of the acropolises and the serene amphitheaters looking over the hills to the sea. Gold and stone, jasper, agates, amethyst, chalcedony, and rock crystal went into the jewels which weighed on the arms, clasped the tunics, and shone in the dyed hair. And in the houses of marble, stone, or wood, and even in the depths of the sepulchers, were seats of marble or of wood, vases of gold, of silver, of bronze, statuettes of terra cotta or of metal, pots of clay or cups of onyx.

The hollow of the hand lent its warmth to precious bits of material, the piece of gold, silver, or copper. Greece did not invent the coin, it is true, but its cities were the first to give it its circular form, to place a head on one side, a symbol on the other, and an inscription composed of watchwords, signatures, or the value. With the diffusion of wealth and aesthetic culture, the coin springs from the bronze matrices in swarms. It is made practically everywhere, in Athens, Asia, Alexandria, and in Sicily especially, in the workshops of Syracuse. Coins mount from the

◀ **The Pergamon Altar,**
frieze of the base in high relief, by Eumenes II, Pergamon,
north side, c. 180 B.C.,
Pergamon Museum in Berlin.

Hellenic hearth like a shower of sparks. The type changes with the city, the events, the victories, and the traditions. Statues, celebrated pictures, legends, myths, symbolic animals, and incisive portraits, the reliefs polished by millions of hands and shaded with black in the hollows have the look of a living material made motionless by the mint. The circle is never a perfect one, the thickness of the disk varies; there, as in other cases, the equilibrium of the elements makes of the art object a complete organism, which symmetry would kill. The metal seems forced out from within as if swelling with juice and with a soul. The Greeks give to it a life of flesh or of the plant. On silver or gold vases they carve networks of twining branches, among which seeds, buds, and leaves — of the oak, the olive tree, the laurel, the plane tree or ivy — seem to tremble. Heavy fruit buries itself in the mystery of the foliage. It is perhaps by these vases and by many of the terra-cotta figurines that we can best judge to what degree the Greeks understood the frame in which the human figure moves. The setting was not a dominant idea with them as it was later on with the Hindus and the men of the Renaissance — especially the Flemings and the Frenchmen of the Renaissance — because the soil of Greece was less rich in animate forms and because the Greeks looked on man as the ripe fruit; it was the fruit that constantly attracted them, whereas the branches, the trunk, and the ground in which the tree grew seemed to them only accompaniments to the superior melody realized by the mind. But their great tragic poets saw the maenads, dressed in tiger skins and girdled with serpents, crowned with flowers and leafy vine branches, bounding out of the forests with the panthers; they spoke of those monstrous unions from which the beast-man came, to affirm the grand accord of indifferent nature and the mind guided by will. And the humblest of their peasants, who knew that the spring and the grotto were peopled with familiar divinities, was at peace as he felt the fraternity of his soil.

Greek Art is preserved until our time, through Pompeii, the perfume of the Greek soul, of which it hands on to us one of the most mysterious aspects, far better than does the art of ceramics, which has traced that soul for us in hardly anything more than its external evolution — in such matters as composition, superficial technique, and subjects. The role of ceramics is limited, with the little terra-cottas, to representing the national industrial art of Greece — which is already saying a good deal. But it cannot pretend to stand for more than the reflection in the popular soul of the flowers gathered by certain minds throughout the nation. Hundreds of workshops had been opened practically everywhere, in Athens, in Sicily, in Etruria, in Cyrenaica, in the Islands, in the Euxine, in a place as distant, even, as the Crimea. The most celebrated painters of cups, Euphronius (late 6th and early 5th centuries BC), Brygos (c. 490 and 470 BC), and Douris (5th c. B. C.), worked with their workmen, often repeated themselves, copied one another and rivaled one another in activity so as to attract patrons. Through the goodly communion of their work, through their continual exchange and emulation, they founded a powerful industry. In it, as in other activities, except where Greece was dominated by Sparta, the slave collaborated with the master, whether as a farmer in the country, as a servant in the city or as an artisan in the workshop; he was, beyond all doubt, less unhappy than the feudal serfs or the wage earner of today. Man was too wise, at that time, to utilize the sufferings of man for his profit; life was too simple, too near the soil, too merged with the light to take the law of hell as its model.

Ares (god of war) and Aphrodite (goddess of love) had their temples, Dionysus also, but outside of Eleusis — a veiled summit, a mysterious region where, doubtless, the unity of our desire was revealed — the three summits of Greece were the Parthenon of Athens, the sanctuary of Delphi, and the Altis of Olympia, where man came to adore Reason, Beauty, and Energy. Heroism is life accepted. It is the progressive and never-attained realization of the conquests that life imposes on us.

Submission to destiny — therein is Greece. There are in Athens, in the little cemetery of Ceramica at the foot of the Acropolis, certain funeral steles of a moving symbolism. Greece so wanted us to love life that she expressed her desire even on the stone of the tomb. Farewells are said there with simple gestures, with slightly sad and perfectly calm faces, as if the persons were going to see each other again.

Alexander fighting the lion together with the Persians, ▶
Alexander sarcophagus, late 4th century B.C.,
marble, h: 69 cm,
Istanbul Archaeology Museum.

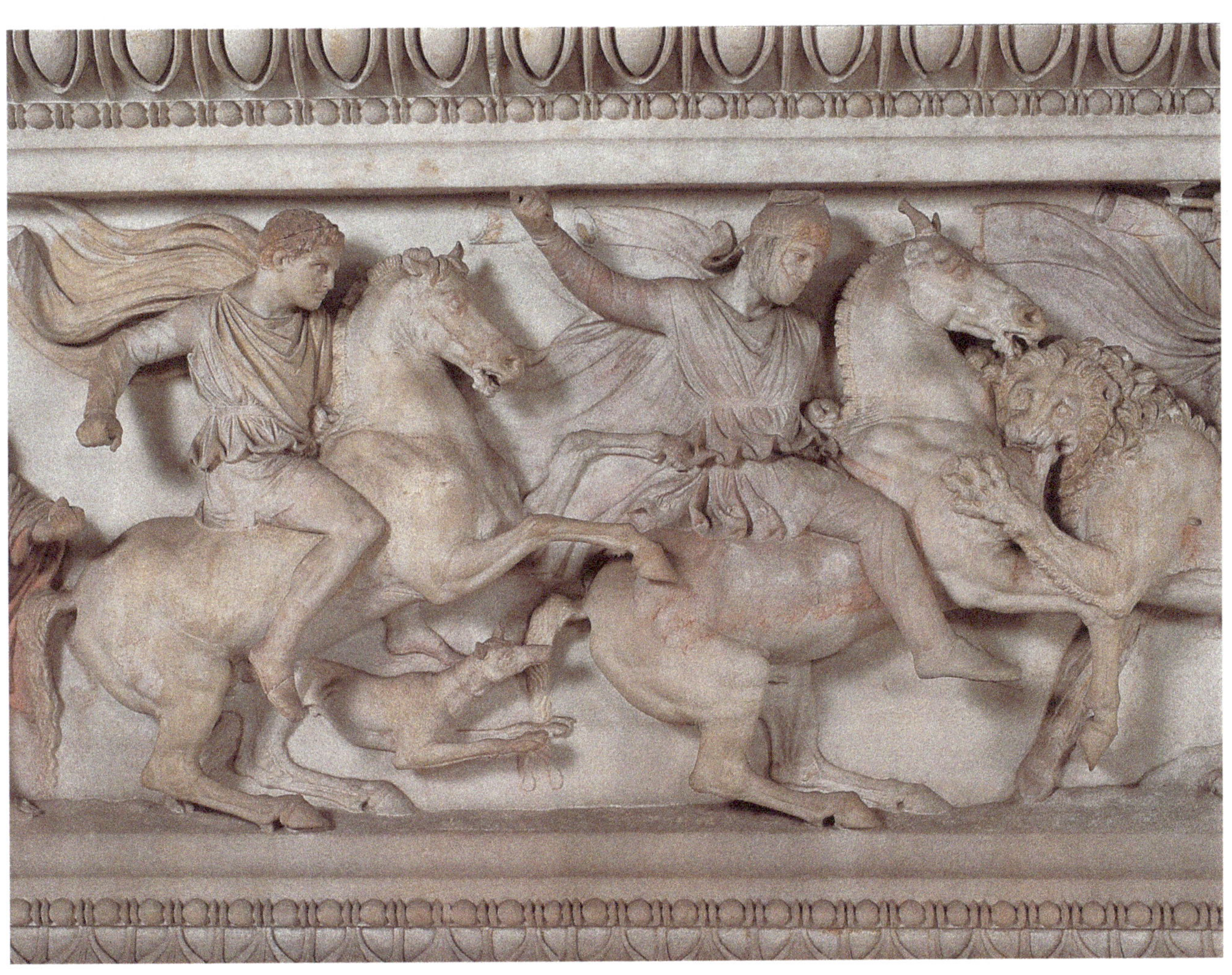